My son was diagnose(
following a Gluten and (
was a pleasure reviewi
taken the time to resear(

GFCF diet and pass along her personal insight. Due to necessity, she is devoted to the book and the other Don't Feed Me products. Thank you, Joyce.

David Kenison, Delano, MN

A book that helps people wade through the daunting prospect of going gluten-free is a wonderful resource to have. There are wonderful recipes to try.

Dr. Kevin Wand, D.O.
Midwest Wellness Center, Bloomington, MN

Finding out your child needs a GFCF diet seems so overwhelming, at first. I wish we had this book 2 years ago. The fact that my mom spent so much time developing this book because of Aivah, and now other children can benefit from it, warms my heart. Aivah definitely has to have the best Nana out there. We hope you enjoy these recipes as much as Aivah does!

Angelica Jenneke, Aivah's mom

By far the most informative and detailed description of gluten-free, dairy-free cooking. The recipes are simple and delicious, even if you're not gluten or dairy intolerant. However, if you are, after reading this book you will come away completely understanding these intolerances and allergies and how to live a healthy, happy life.

Erin Paulsen, B.A., M.S.

I would like to thank my family for encouraging me, always believing in me and for tasting my "creations" – good and bad. And thank you, Aivah. You truly are an inspiration!

I would like to give a special thanks to David Kenison for his support, professional advice and for encouraging me to go beyond my comfort zone.

Visit us at

www.dontfeedme.com

send us an email at

info@dontfeedme.com

We are all angels with one wing – we need each other to fly.

Anonymous

Inspiration

I was inspired to write this cookbook when my granddaughter, Aivah, was diagnosed with Celiac disease and a casein allergy at age 14 months. Anyone who has had any experience with gluten intolerance or a gluten allergy will be able to understand what we went through before her diagnosis. Our journey to find healthy, nutritious foods to feed a small child began with her diagnosis. It has been a frustrating and enlightening experience.

Since Aivah has a casein allergy in addition to a gluten allergy, we had to find recipes that were gluten-free and dairy-free. We found "dairy-free" recipes, but they contained gluten. We found "gluten-free" recipes, but they contained dairy. It was a struggle to find recipes with NO dairy and NO gluten.

There are a large number of dairy-free cookbooks on the market, but most of these recipes include wheat flour and other types of gluten. There are also a number of gluten-free cookbooks - that use a lot of milk, cream and cheese in their recipes. I couldn't seem to find gluten-free AND dairy-free in one recipe.

A lot of the gluten-free cookbooks mention that many Celiacs are also lactose intolerant or have problems with dairy products. If this is the case, I am curious as to why so many gluten-free recipes include dairy. It sounds simple when the cookbooks tell me I can substitute a non-dairy product for the dairy called for in a recipe. Unfortunately, soy and rice milk don't always substitute equally for cow's milk. On occasion, they will alter the flavor of the cooked food. There are times when other compensations or additions need to be made when using soy or rice products. Soy and rice cheese doesn't melt or taste the same as dairy cheese. I have also found you can substitute chicken broth for milk in many of the recipes, for an entirely different flavor.

Another problem we had with the gluten-free and dairy-free cookbooks on the market was that many of the recipes were aimed toward adult tastes. Recipes for foods such as Chili Rellenos, salads with capers and spicy dishes were normal. Thai food and Tequila-lime shrimp are wonderful recipes - for adults or older children. My 14 month old granddaughter wasn't ready for this type of food. She wanted meat, potatoes, vegetables, breads (she LOVES her bread!) and sweets.

My search for gluten-free and dairy-free recipes is what prompted me to write this cookbook. This cookbook is meant to give you a basic understanding of the gluten-free, dairy-free diet. I have$_3$ covered the different ingredients, what they do, how they taste and how to combine them into tasty, nutritious meals that will satisfy anyone from small child to adult. If you are new to the diet, it can be very confusing and at times overwhelming. So much to remember, so many new ingredients and the way you are used to cooking is pretty much out the window!

I have had problems with dairy for over 10 years. My daughter Annie, Aivah's mom, has had problems with dairy for most of her life. After she had her last child, Aivah, her intolerance to dairy became more pronounced. When Aivah was a month old, Annie noticed Aivah would get abdominal cramps and diarrhea shortly after she nursed her. This didn't happen every time, just occasionally. I told her to think about what she had eaten up to 8 hours before nursing Aivah. Whatever the mother eats or drinks DOES pass through breast milk to the baby. Through much trial and error, Annie discovered each time she drank milk or ate a milk product Aivah would suffer as much as she did. Since Annie had problems with dairy, it wasn't difficult for her to stop all dairy products while she was nursing Aivah. As Aivah grew and started eating solid food, Annie fed her a dairy-free diet.

The signs and symptoms of casein allergy were fairly easy to spot in Aivah. My daughter and I have years of experience with reactions to dairy. She would occasionally try dairy products on Aivah and found she had a severe reaction each time. Aivah's doctor agreed she didn't have a lactose intolerance but a casein allergy. She couldn't tolerate any dairy without suffering severe bloating, gas and diarrhea. Lactose intolerance refers to a person's inability to digest lactose. Lactose is a sugar found in milk. A casein allergy is the body's allergic reaction to casein. Casein is a protein in milk.

Annie removed all dairy from Aivah's diet. When you remove an entire food group from someone's diet, you need to be sure to substitute other foods to replace the vitamins and nutrients missing from not eating dairy products. Soy and rice milks are fortified with the same necessary vitamins and minerals found in dairy milk, without the lactose or casein. We found Aivah preferred soy milk over rice milk. Annie also included more foods rich in calcium and magnesium. Your body needs magnesium to absorb calcium.

Finding non-dairy foods for Aivah was challenging but not overwhelming. There are many products made with soy and rice that are nutritious and tasty. We found a vegan cheese that actually melts – which is very important when making the childhood standby – macaroni and cheese. We wanted Aivah to be able to eat the same types of meals as the rest of the family. Foods like macaroni and cheese, pudding, ice cream, grilled cheese, hot dogs, pies and cakes are part of childhood. We didn't want her to feel like she was different, or that her diet was limited. She was able to eat the same food as the rest of the family. We just had to prepare it a little differently.

As Aivah grew, Annie introduced more foods into her diet. Aivah loved her peanut butter sandwiches. Aivah grew, but didn't seem to thrive the way she should. She was a little bitty thing and was on the low end of the height and weight chart. When Aivah was feeling bad, one of the things that made her happy was a peanut butter sandwich. She began having bouts of severe gas and diarrhea, again. Occasionally, she would have unexplained rashes on her abdomen and buttocks. Sometimes, she would get diaper rash so bad it would bleed. Annie took many trips to the doctor to see if they could determine what was wrong. Aivah was tested for many childhood illnesses and diseases. All the results were negative.

Finally, at 14 months old, Aivah was diagnosed with a gluten allergy. Unfortunately, it wasn't an immediate diagnosis (nothing ever is).

Since Aivah was so little, she couldn't tell us what, where or why she hurt. Her symptoms mirrored the symptoms of many other childhood illnesses and diseases. There were months of irritability, hours of screaming, foul-smelling diarrhea, hours of screaming, red blotchy hives that covered her entire body, hours of screaming, abdominal cramps, headaches (yes, babies can get headaches. She used to hit both sides of her head with her fists, shake her head and scream for hours), high fevers, terrible diaper rash that would sometimes bleed, - oh , did I mention hours of screaming???

After buckets and buckets of tears (Aivah's, her mom's AND myself), numerous trips to the doctor, trips to the emergency room, blood tests, allergy tests, doses of penicillin (we discovered she also has an allergy to penicillin) with no diagnosis, we decided to try a few of our own "food allergy tests". We both knew that many food allergies can be misdiagnosed.

Since many people who have a gluten intolerance or gluten allergy are also lactose intolerant or have a casein allergy, we started there. Perhaps her reaction to dairy made itself known first, since she ate dairy foods before she ate gluten foods. The first thing we did was$_5$ stopped giving her bread - which did not make her happy! She loved her peanut butter sandwiches!

Then we started researching gluten - what it is, what it does to those who have an intolerance or allergy to it, what food it's hidden in, what other names it's called. It was a frustrating and informative time.

As soon as we removed the bread from her diet, we saw an improvement. She was happier, played more and wasn't as listless as she had been. And she screamed less - a LOT less (thank you!). She still had times when she had a lot of abdominal cramping, liquid diarrhea and headaches.

Because there was such a drastic improvement by just removing bread, we decided to put her on an entirely gluten-free diet, with her doctor's approval. After just two weeks on the diet, she was a completely new child. She was happy, full of energy, without headaches, had normal BM's and she developed a funny sense of humor. This convinced us to stick with the gluten-free diet.

Thankfully, Aivah had a pediatrician who was willing to listen to my daughter, Annie, and was open to different ideas. He ran a few tests on her blood and stool samples. If necessary, he was ready to perform an intestinal biopsy, which is the standard technique to diagnose celiac disease. With the drastic improvement on the gluten-free diet, he didn't feel it was necessary to put a 15 month old child through that surgery.

Switching to a gluten-free diet was not a matter of just removing bread from Aivah's diet. A large percentage of packaged foods are manufactured with gluten. Unfortunately, not all gluten is called "gluten" or "flour". Chapter 2 lists other names for gluten you need to watch for. We adopted a new house rule - "Never put anything in her mouth until you read the ingredients first." We also taught Aivah that certain foods would give her "owies" in her tummy. For someone so little, she developed a very good understanding of what she could and couldn't eat.

We also had to be very careful not to contaminate her food with gluten from the rest of the family's food, which can be a challenge. We discovered something as simple as making a peanut butter sandwich required double steps. We needed two loaves of bread (one wheat and one gluten-free). We needed two knives (the knife that touches the wheat bread cannot touch the gluten-free bread - or gluten-free margarine or gluten-free peanut butter), two containers of margarine, two containers of peanut butter and two cutting boards.

Cross-contamination is something that is very easy to do. If you place a slice of wheat bread on the counter, the counter is contaminated with gluten. You can't see it, but it's there. It's easy to be conscious of where the bread is placed - but let's not forget gluten is also in artificial flavors, caramel color, spices - any number of hidden places. You can't cook non-gluten foods in the same pan that you cook gluten-containing foods. If you do, you need to cook the non-gluten foods first and remove them from the pan before you cook the gluten foods. I'll admit, it sounds a little overwhelming. So much to remember - who put what where, did I read the ingredients, where did they hide the gluten this time?

My daughter has seven children. At the time of Aivah's diagnosis their ages were 14, 10, 7, 6, 4, 3 and 14 months, with Aivah as the last one. In addition to learning all the new "rules" ourselves, we also had to teach the other children about gluten, cross-contamination and being VERY careful with their own food. Since most children can't seem to eat without dropping or spilling something, there was always the chance that some surface could be contaminated with gluten.

At first, I'm sure my grandchildren got tired of hearing me say, "If you take it out, put it away," or "If you see something on the (** insert floor, counter, chair, etc.) pick it up, even if you didn't put it there" and "If you make a mess clean it up." We explained to them what gluten was, where it was found and how sick their baby sister could get from the smallest amount of gluten. They had seen her screaming in pain and many of them had helped change her diapers when her gluten reaction was at its worst. They didn't want to see her go through that again. Training everyone to be conscious of gluten contamination was the most difficult part.

I have been involved with special diets for over 30 years. In the '70's, when my oldest daughter, Erin, was four years old, she was diagnosed with what they called "hyperactivity". Today, the diagnosis would probably be ADHD. The idea of controlling her behavior with medication did not appeal to me. I began my search for alternative methods of treatment. Keep in mind, this was before computers and the internet. All my research was done at the library. I read thousands of pages in hundreds of books. After much research, the route I chose to take was to remove all refined sugars, artificial colors, artificial flavors and preservatives from her diet. The results were amazing. Before her diet change, she would have periods where she just couldn't sit still. She would talk a mile a minute and would rush from one toy to another. It was as if she had a motor inside that was stuck on high speed. If I gave her a piece of candy you could see the drastic change in her behavior within minutes. She would be calmly sitting down, reading a book (yes, she read at 4 years old). She would eat the small piece of candy. Within minutes her foot would start tapping, then her legs couldn't be still. She would wiggle and squirm in her seat. She would get up and walk around, then run and literally bounce off the walls! This would go on for an hour or more before she would start to wind down and crash. Once I adjusted her diet, we no longer had the extreme behavioral highs and lows. She was just a "normal" kid.

Back in the '70's we didn't have "natural" or "organic" stores where I lived. Nor was this type of food available in chain grocery stores, as it is today. Everything had to be made from scratch. I learned to make fruit roll ups, crackers, bread, cakes, cookies and candy. It took a little more time than opening a box to cook dinner, but it was so much healthier and better for both my children. I didn't need to put my daughter on chemical drugs at such a young age, either.

My youngest daughter, Annie, has had difficulty digesting dairy products most of her life. As she got older and began having her own children, her intolerance to dairy increased. I have helped her learn how to cook dairy-free and still get enough nutrients from other foods. Annie continued to try various dairy foods throughout the years. At times, she considers it worth the consequence in order to eat something with dairy in it. Most of the time, the knowledge of what she will go through stops her from eating dairy

When I reached my 40's, I began to have problems with dairy. I assumed I was also lactose intolerant and removed diary from my diet. On occasion, I would try dairy products to see what would happen. I discovered I could eat organic dairy products - milk, cheese, cream, etc. – and not suffer any symptoms. Yet, when I ate commercial dairy products, I would have the severe abdominal cramping, diarrhea, gas, etc. After almost 8 years of "trial and error", and a doctor willing to listen to my ideas, I discovered I am not lactose intolerant – I am chemically intolerant. I have severe reactions to MSG, sodium nitrate, sodium nitrite and petroleum based products. Apparently there is some chemical that is used in processing commercial milk, or that is in the feed given to the dairy cows that I can't tolerate.

There are so many chemicals out there that it is impossible for me to narrow it down to one chemical. It is easier to just avoid commercial dairy products. I also avoid non-food products (such as soaps, lotions, toothpaste, etc.) that are petroleum based. Researching the "other names" for petroleum was another research project. Since this is a book about gluten-free, dairy-free cooking I won't go into detail.

When you start cooking for someone with a special diet, it can be overwhelming. Even the basics have to be changed. So many of us are used to using packaged foods (foods that include the things you can no longer eat) that you may feel like you have to start from scratch again in learning how to cook. I've included instructions for basic foods in this book for things such as rice and potatoes. It does take a little longer to prepare meals from scratch, rather than opening a box and adding water, but it is worth the few extra minutes. Your food will be healthier and so will you.

Hopefully, the information and recipes in this book will help you realize that a gluten-free, dairy-free diet is not impossible or restrictive. You can still eat the foods you're used to – you just need to use a few different ingredients and perhaps change the way you prepare it.

There are many gluten-free recipes available. If you search for gluten-free recipes on the internet you will find many, many recipes. There are also many dairy-free recipes available. The recipes in this book are ones I use on a regular basis. Some of them are a combination of gluten-free and/or dairy-free recipes that we adjusted to suit our tastes. Many of the recipes are old family favorites that I have converted to be gluten-free and dairy-free.

The journey to these recipes has been a long road of trial and error littered with some really bad food! Thankfully, the trials also produced quite a few successful recipes. I hope the recipes in this cookbook will help you if you have a need to cook gluten-free and dairy-free. I welcome and appreciate your comments and suggestions. Feel free to e-mail me at info@dontfeedme.com.

To the left is Aivah at age 14 months.

This is before her diagnosis.

To the right is Aivah only 2 weeks later on a strict gluten-free, dairy-free diet.

CHAPTER 1

Gluten Intolerance/Allergy Symptoms

The symptoms of a gluten allergy or intolerance (Celiac disease) are a result of the inability of the small intestine to absorb nutrients from food as it is digested. Gluten is a protein found in grains such as wheat, oats, barley and others. Gluten causes damage to the villi of the small intestine and can lead to malnutrition. Villi are small, finger-like projections in the small intestines that absorb nutrients as the food passes through. Gluten causes damage by irritating, flattening and shortening the villi. Damaged villi cannot absorb nutrients, resulting in malabsorption of nutrients and malnutrition. Basically, the food your child eats is going in one end and out the other without stopping to leave behind the necessary vitamins, minerals and calories for proper nutrition. The small intestine is where iron, folic acid, calcium and Vitamins K, A, D and E are absorbed.

Some possible symptoms of a gluten allergy and/or intolerance are:

Blistered rashes on stomach, buttocks, arms, legs
 (The medical term for this is Dermatitis Herpetiformis - DH)

Liquid, foul-smelling diarrhea	Headache
Distended abdomen	Weight loss
Lack of muscle definition	High fever
Abdominal cramping	Flatulence (gas)
Vomiting (at times projectile vomiting)	Listlessness
Inability to sleep through the night	Constipation
Dark circles under the eyes	Anemia
Low height and weight gain	Irritability

Unfortunately, the above symptoms can also be caused by other illnesses and diseases. If your child has a number of the above symptoms for any length of time, please consult with their doctor.

If left untreated, a gluten allergy and/or intolerance can cause permanent damage to the small intestine. It can become life-threatening and can cause other conditions such as:

Central and peripheral nervous system disorders
Osteoporosis and other bone diseases
Lack of dental enamel formation
Delayed start in menstruation
ADD / ADHD type symptoms
Internal hemorrhaging
Weight loss
Anemia

CHAPTER 2

Gluten
by any other name . . .

Other Names for Gluten

Gluten is a special type of protein that is found in many grains. Gluten helps make baked goods elastic, giving it that "chewy" texture. This is why you need to add xanthan gum or guar gum to baked goods made with gluten-free flours. Without one of these ingredients, your baked goods won't hold together.

Gluten can be found in many foods. Everyone recognizes "wheat flour" or "flour". This is not a complete list, but a list of the most commonly used names for gluten:

Alcohol
Artificial colors
Barley
Blue cheese
Bran
Caramel color
Couscous
Dextrimaltose
Dextrins
Edible starch
Glucose syrup
Groats
Hydrolyzed wheat protein
Hydrolyzed wheat gluten
Hydrolyzed wheat starch
Hydroxypropyltrimonium
Kamut
Malt (flavoring, extract, syrup)
Miso
Modified food starch
MSG (Monosodium Glutamate)
Maltodextrin
Maltos

Oats
Semsiline
Soy sauce
Smoke flavoring
Starch
Tabbouleh
Teriyaki sauce
Triticum Aestirum
Triticale (a hybrid of wheat & rye)
Vegetable starch
Wheat starch
Wheat protein
Wheat germ
Wine

CHAPTER 3

Dairy Intolerance/Allergy Symptoms

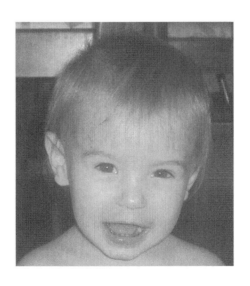

Lactose Intolerance refers to a person's inability to digest lactose, the sugar found in milk. Lactose intolerance is caused by a deficiency of the enzyme lactase, which is produced by the cells lining the small intestine. Lactase breaks down lactose into two simpler forms of sugar called glucose and galactose, which are then absorbed into the bloodstream. Lactose makes up about 2 – 8% of milk.

Casein (milk protein) allergy refers to the body's allergic reaction to casein. People sometimes confuse lactose intolerance with casein allergy. An allergy occurs when our body's immune system reacts to the proteins in cow's milk, casein and whey, as if they were a foreign substance. Casein allergy can be life threatening when just a small amount of milk or milk product is consumed.

Milk is made up of water, protein (casein and whey), carbohydrates (a milk sugar called lactose), minerals, fats and other substances. Casein allergy is often apparent with babies, but can remain undiagnosed until adulthood. Recent evidence indicates that up to *75% of the world's population is Lactose Intolerant* to some extent. That is, three quarters (¾) of all people have difficulty digesting lactose.

Symptoms of **lactose intolerance** and/or **casein allergy** can affect the skin, the digestive tract and the respiratory system.

Symptoms of Lactose Intolerance or Casein Allergy can include:

Runny nose	Asthma
Vomiting	Hives and rashes
Eczema	Diarrhea
Hyperactive behavior	Ear infections
Bloating	Watery eyes
Flatulence (gas)	Dark circles around the eyes
Recurrent bronchitis	Failure to thrive
Malabsorption of nutrients (anemia)	

If you or your child experience a number of the above symptoms, consult with their doctor.

CHAPTER 4

Dairy
by any other name . . .

Other Names for Dairy

Dairy can be found in many foods. Everyone recognizes "milk", "cream" and "butter". This is not a complete list, but other sources of dairy may be found in or called:

Ammonium
Calcium Caseinate
Casein
Caseinate
Delactosen Whey
Demineralized Whey
Hydrolyzed Casein
Hydrolyzed Milk Protein
Hydrolyzed Whey
Iron Caseinate
Lactalbamin
Lactagloulin Phosphate
Lactate
Lactic Acid
Lactoferrin
Lactose
Magnesium Caseinate
Milk Solids
Rennet
Opta
Potassium Caseinate
Sodium Caseinate
Whey
Whey protein
Zinc Caseinate

If you can't eat dairy products, you need to be sure you are getting enough calcium, Vitamin D and magnesium in your diet. (magnesium helps your body absorb calcium).

Other sources of calcium include:

Soy milk, fortified	1 cup	447 grams
Sesame seeds	¼ cup	351 grams
Fortified gluten-free cereal	1 cup	300 grams
Fortified orange juice	1 cup	297 grams
Spinach, cooked	1 cup	245 grams
Spinach, fresh	1 cup	350 grams
Collard greens, boiled	1 cup	226 grams
Turnip greens, cooked	1 cup	226 grams
Soybeans, cooked	1 cup	180 grams
Broccoli, fresh	1 cup	180 grams
Broccoli, steamed	1 cup	75 grams
Almonds	2 oz	150 grams
Navy beans	1 cup	130 grams
Black beans	1 cup	120 grams
Tofu, raw	4 oz	100 grams
Bok Choy	1 cup	160 grams
Green beans, steamed	1 cup	60 grams
Cinnamon, ground	2 tsp	56 grams
Brussels sprouts, boiled	1 cup	56 grams
Thyme, dried, ground	2 tsp	54 grams
Oranges	1 each	52 grams
Garlic	1 oz	51 grams
Summer squash, cooked	1 cup	49 grams
Celery, raw	1 cup	48 grams
Oregano, dried, ground	2 tsp	47 grams
Cabbage, shredded	1 cup	47 grams
Romaine lettuce	2 cups	40 grams
Asparagus, steamed	1 cup	36 grams

CHAPTER 5

Non-Gluten Flours

Arrowroot Flour

This is a white flour that is ground from the root of the Arrowroot plant. It can be exchanged for cornstarch.

Aramanth Flour

This flour is ground from the Aramanth seed. It is related to pigweed.

Brown Rice Flour

This is milled from unpolished brown rice and is higher in nutrients than white rice flour.

Buckwheat Flour

Despite the name, buckwheat flour is not a wheat grain. It is related to rhubarb. It has a very strong flavor and is normally used in very small quantities.

Cornstarch

This is a refined starch from corn. It can be used to thicken liquids. If you are allergic to corn, replace with arrowroot or potato starch.

Cornmeal

This grainy meal is ground from corn. You can purchase yellow or white cornmeal.

Corn Flour

This flour is milled from corn and its consistency is that of other flours, not grainy.

Garbanzo Bean Flour

This flour is ground from garbanzo beans (also called chickpeas). It is high in protein.

Garfava Flour
This is a combination of garbanzo beans and fava beans. It is not as grainy as rice flour and is high in protein.

Millet Flour
Millet is a grain in the same family as corn, rice & sorghum. This flour has been accepted in Canada as gluten-free for many years. It is being accepted by many gluten-free groups in the US now.

Potato Flour
This is a heavy flour and is normally used in small quantities.

Potato Starch Flour
Do not confuse potato flour with potato starch flour. This flour is a fine white flour. I use this in many of the recipes in this book.

Quinoa Flour (pronounced "kin-wa")
Made from Quinoa seeds and is related to spinach and beets. The plant has a bitter tasting coating, so always buy debittered quinoa flour. Quinoa flour has been accepted in Canada as gluten-free. Many US groups are accepting that this flour is not linked to grains that contain gluten.

Sorghum Flour
This flour is milled from the sorghum grain. It has a strong flavor and is normally combined with other flours.

Soy Flour
This is a yellow flour with a nutty flavor. It is high in protein. It is normally combined with other bland flours.

Tapioca Flour
This flour is made from the root of the cassava plant. It is a light, white flour. It gives texture to baked goods. This is a staple at our house.

Tef (Teff) Flour

Tef is a grain in the same family as corn, rice & sorghum. Tef flour has been accepted in Canada as gluten-free. Many US groups are accepting that this flour is not linked to grains that contain gluten.

White Rice Flour

This is milled from polished white rice and is very bland in taste. It has been a basic in gluten-free baking. Since it tends to add a grainy texture to baked goods, I combine it with other softer flours.

FLOURS TO AVOID

Bulger, Club, Durum, Einkorn, Kamut, Semolina and Spelt

These are all various species of wheat and should not be eaten in any form by anyone following a gluten-free diet.

Oats

Some Canadian groups have accepted oats on a gluten-free diet. It can cause problems for many, because of the high risk of cross-contamination from other grains. I would suggest you try a small amount to see if you can tolerate oats. We avoid it in Aivah's diet.

Triticale

This is a hybrid grain that is a combination of rye and wheat and should not be eaten by those following a gluten-free diet. Watch for this grain when reading ingredients on packaged goods.

INGREDIENTS NECESSARY FOR GLUTEN-FREE COOKING

Corn Starch
This is used for thickening sauces and gravies, and in combination with flours in baking.

Dough Enhancers
These are powdered products used in making bread. You can use them to replace the vinegar called for in recipes. Vinegar is readily available and low in cost.

Dry Milk Powder
Some recipes (not mine) call for dry milk powder. Use it if you are able to tolerate dairy. There is also a soy milk powder on the market you can use.

Gelatin Powder
This adds moisture and protein to foods. It helps to hold ingredients together.

Guar Gum
It can be used in place of xanthan gum, but can cause intestinal distress. Guar gum has a high fiber content and is also sold as a laxative. Use sparingly.

Xanthan Gum
This replaces gluten in yeast breads and is used as a thickener in many recipes. It helps prevent crumbling.

Yeast
Fresh yeast is the key to successful breads and foods that need to rise. Don't use the rapid-rise yeast unless the recipe specifically calls for it.

CHAPTER 6

Cross-Contamination

Cross-contamination occurs when a gluten-free food comes in contact with a food that contains gluten, or with a surface where a food containing gluten was placed. Cross-contamination is a very real problem for those who follow a gluten-free diet. If you choose to cook gluten foods and non-gluten foods in the same kitchen, as we do, there are steps you need to take to avoid cross contaminating the non-gluten foods.

Gluten is invisible to the naked eye, but can contaminate surfaces such as counters and cutting boards very easily. A good example is making two peanut butter sandwiches. One sandwich is with gluten bread and the other is with gluten-free bread.

You make the peanut butter sandwich with gluten bread, first. You set the two slices of bread on the counter. You then spread the margarine and peanut butter on the gluten bread. Using the same knife, you cut the sandwich in half and place the halves on a plate. You remove the knife you used, the margarine and the jar of peanut butter. Now you are ready to make the gluten-free peanut butter sandwich.

You take out the gluten-free margarine, the gluten free peanut butter, the gluten-free bread and a new knife. You set the bread on the counter . . . and you've just contaminated the gluten-free bread with the gluten that is on the counter from the previous sandwich.

If you are going to make the sandwiches on toast you will need two separate toasters. Once you place a slice of gluten bread in the toaster, it is contaminated and cannot be used for gluten-free bread.

It is not necessary to purchase a new set of pots, baking pans and utensils to use for gluten-free cooking. However, you do need to pay close attention to how you take care of the pans and utensils you do use. A thorough washing of pots, pans and utensils will remove the gluten from them. I would suggest you use separate wooden spoons since the gluten can be absorbed into the wood.

If you use plastic containers to store leftovers, you will need to keep the containers for the gluten and gluten-free foods separate. Plastic can absorb gluten and contaminate any food you store in it. Be sure to mark the gluten-free containers clearly.

Foods that will not be consumed in one serving, such as margarine, peanut butter and honey, need to be kept separate. If you use a knife to spread margarine or peanut butter onto gluten bread, the knife is contaminated and cannot be put back in the margarine or peanut butter container without contaminating the entire container.

The same rules apply to gluten-free flours. Do not store them in the same cupboard as the gluten flours. We have a separate cupboard for Aivah's gluten-free flours, xanthan gum, sugars and yeast packages to avoid any chance of contamination. We also have a separate area in the refrigerator for her gluten-free breads and other gluten-free foods to avoid contamination.

Cross-contamination is a problem when eating in restaurants. A restaurant may advertise that they offer gluten-free foods – but if they cook their gluten-free foods alongside the gluten foods, your gluten-free foods will be contaminated. If they use the same utensils on both gluten and non-gluten foods, your food is no longer gluten free. It may be made with gluten-free ingredients, yet contaminated with gluten from the other foods, cooking surfaces or utensils. Many people can understand that a food needs to be prepared with gluten-free ingredients. Yet they don't understand the cross-contamination issues. Always check where the restaurant is cooking the gluten-free foods.

CHAPTER 7

Finding
Gluten and Dairy
Information

First and foremost – **READ THE INGREDIENTS!** Manufacturers change the ingredients in their products from time to time. A product that was gluten-free, or dairy-free, the last time you bought it may contain gluten, or dairy, the next time you buy it.

You also need to remember that even though a product is listed as gluten-free, it must also be manufactured in a gluten-free plant to be truly gluten-free. Many manufacturers make products with gluten-free and/or dairy-free ingredients, but also manufacture products that contain gluten or dairy in the same plant. If so, there is a risk of cross-contamination. To be truly gluten-free and dairy-free, a food must be manufactured in a separate area where there is no chance of cross-contamination. Many companies state on their labels that the food is manufactured in the same plant as gluten and/or dairy products. Unfortunately, not all companies do this.

The best way to find out if a product contains dairy or gluten or is manufactured in a gluten-free or dairy-free facility, is to call the manufacturer and ask. You may have to talk to a few people to get to the right department, but it is well worth the effort.

Food isn't the only thing to be concerned with. Products such as toothpaste, lotions, shampoos, band-aids and medicines can also contain dairy or gluten. Gluten products are used as thickeners. Dried milk and/or dairy solids are commonly found in hair and body products. READ INGREDIENTS before purchasing anything. Believe me, this becomes second nature. Each time you pick up something, you automatically turn it to the ingredient listing before you consider purchasing it. ☺

We have found many products that are gluten-free and dairy-free. I am not able to mention them by brand name in this book, but the easiest way to know if a product is gluten-free or dairy-free is to either go to the company website or call the company directly. There are also many gluten-free lists available via the internet that state specific brand names. Remember to continue to read ingredient lists to be sure the manufacturers haven't changed their ingredients.

We have found many gluten-free products that we use regularly. Because of legal and trademark restrictions, I am not able to mention most of them in this cookbook.

I received permission from two companies (at the time of printing) to mention their products in my cookbook. Karo® light corn syrup is gluten-free. (Karo® is a registered trademark of ACH Food Companies, Inc.) Lawry's Seasoned Salt and McCormick single ingredient spices are also gluten-free. These products are quality products and remain gluten-free.

As always – it is up to those following the gluten-free, dairy-free diet to determine if a product is safe for them.

CHAPTER 8

Breakfast

Breakfast Frittata

Serves 4

1/2 C soy milk
4 eggs
1 C unpeeled potatoes, diced
1/2 C chopped celery
10 - 15 fresh spinach leaves
2 Tbl GF, DF margarine
1 tsp Lawry's seasoned salt
1/4 tsp black pepper
1/2 tsp dried basil

In a small bowl combine eggs, milk, basil, salt and pepper. Mix thoroughly. Set aside

In large oven-proof frying pan (cast iron works best) melt GF margarine over medium heat. Add potatoes and celery. Sprinkle with GF seasoned salt. Cook over medium heat, stirring occasionally, until potatoes are tender and slightly browned. Add onion and cook 5 minutes until onions are soft. Lay spinach leaves over top of potato mixture, covering completely but leaving 1/2 inch open around edge.

Stir egg mixture to combine and pour over contents in frying pan. Cook for 5 minutes, lifting edges so egg mixture run under frittata. Place pan under broiler. Broil 5 minutes until top is puffy and browned. Remove from broiler. Cut into pie shaped slices and serve immediately.

Suggestion
If you don't have an oven-proof pan, when edges are cooked and center is slightly liquid, lift edge of mixture to loosen and pour 4 Tbl water around edge. Cover immediately and cook on low heat for 5 minutes until center is cooked through. The steam created from the water will cook the top and center of the Frittata.

Add one or more of the following:
   1/2 cup cooked chicken or turkey
   1/2 cup broccoli florets
   1 small can green chilies

Add 1 egg for each 1 cup additional ingredients added.

Cream of Rice Cereal

Serves 1

1/2 C cream of rice cereal
1 C water
1/2 C soy milk
1 tsp granulated sugar
1/4 tsp cinnamon

Place water and rice cereal in small saucepan. Cook on medium heat, stirring constantly, until mixture starts to thicken (about 5 minutes). Remove from heat. Spoon cereal into bowl. Add milk, sugar and cinnamon. Stir until combined.

Suggestions:

* Add fresh sliced strawberries, blueberries or blackberries to cooked cereal.

* Replace 1 tsp sugar with 1 Tbl honey or 1 tsp GF brown sugar

The most important things in life aren't things.

Anthony D'Angelo

Breakfast Pizza

Serves 4

1 GF Pizza Crust recipe
  (page 60)
2 tsp vegetable oil
½ lb ground turkey or beef
¼ C chopped onion
1 C GF frozen hash browns,
        thawed
1 C dairy-free cheese chunks
1 tsp Lawry's seasoned salt
4 eggs
¼ C soy milk
¼ tsp pepper

Cut dairy-free cheese into small pieces, or shred.

Follow GF pizza crust recipe to the point where you pre-bake the crust. Bake pizza crust for 5 minutes, then remove from oven and set aside while you prepare the topping ingredients.

In large skillet combine oil, ground turkey (or beef), onion, seasoned salt and pepper. Cook over medium heat, stirring occasionally, until turkey is cooked.

Sprinkle turkey, hash browns and cheese over pizza crust.

In a medium bowl, beat eggs and soy milk. Pour egg mixture over pizza.

Bake for 20 – 25 minutes or until golden brown. Let stand 5 minutes before cutting.

Breakfast Tortilla

Serves 4 - 6

1-16 oz can refried beans
½ C GF salsa
2 Tbl GF, DF margarine
5 eggs
½ C soy milk
1 C dairy-free cheese
½ tsp Lawry's seasoned salt
¼ tsp pepper
¼ tsp GF cumin
8 GF tortillas
1 C shredded lettuce

In a small saucepan, mix refried beans and salsa over medium heat. When heated through, turn heat to low to keep warm.

In small bowl, beat eggs, soy milk and seasonings.

Heat margarine in large skillet, until melted. Pour eggs into skillet. Heat and stir until eggs are cooked through.

Sprinkle top of eggs with cheese. Remove from heat, cover and set aside. Cheese will melt from heat.

To serve:

Spread each tortilla with 1 – 2 Tbl of refried bean/salsa mixture. Top with 2 – 3 Tbl egg mixture and shredded lettuce. Fold ¼ of tortilla over mixture (this will be the bottom). Fold each side over filling and eat.

Streusel Topped Coffee Cake

Serves 8

½ C rice flour
½ C tapioca flour
½ C potato starch flour
¼ C vegetable oil
2 eggs
½ C soy milk
1½ tsp xanthan gum
1 C granulated sugar
2 tsp GF baking powder

Streusel Topping

½ C GF brown sugar
2 Tbl tapioca flour
2 tsp GF cinnamon
3 Tbl melted GF, DF margarine

Preheat oven to 350 degrees.

Grease an 8″ x 8″ square or round cake pan.

In large bowl combine oil, eggs and soy milk.

In medium bowl combine flours, xanthan gum, sugar and baking powder.

Add the dry ingredients to the egg mixture and stir well to combine.

Pour batter into prepared pan. Set aside.

In small bowl mix streusel topping ingredients. Use fingers to sprinkle topping over top of batter.

Bake for 25 minutes or until toothpick inserted in center comes out clean.

Toad in a Hole

Serves 4

4 slices GF bread
  (Soft White Bread works well)
4 Tbl GFF margarine
4 eggs
salt & pepper to taste

Heat large frying pan or griddle over medium heat.

While pan is heating, spread GF margarine on both sides of each slice of bread. Cut a hole in the center of each slice of bread - about 2" across.

Put bread slices on griddle. Break one egg into hole in each slice of bread. White part of egg will spread across top of bread. Cook about 2 minutes, until bottom of bread is brown. Flip each slice of bread and cook additional 2 minutes until egg white is cooked and yolk is still soft. (If you prefer a hard yolk, cook additional minute).

Transfer "toads" onto plates and salt and pepper to taste.

Laugh as much as you breathe and love as long as you live.

Anonymous

Frozen Breakfast

Serves 4

1-15 oz can crushed pineapple
4 bananas, sliced
1-15 oz can peaches in juice
2-10oz pkg frozen strawberries
with juice
1 C granulated sugar

Drain pineapple and reserve juice for other recipes or drink.

Drain peaches and reserve juice for this recipe.

In large bowl combine pineapple, banana slices, peach slices and strawberries with juice.

In small saucepan combine peach juice and sugar. Bring to a boil over medium heat. Boil for 2 minutes and remove from heat.

Pour peach syrup over fruits in bowl. Stir gently to combine.

Spoon fruit into cupcake cups lined with paper liners. Place in freezer for 2 hours or overnight.

Allow fruit cups to sit at room temperatures for 10 minutes before serving. Serve in paper cups or invert onto plate and remove cupcake paper.

Hash Brown Breakfast Pie

Serves 4

3 C GF frozen hash browns
1/3 C GF, DF margarine, melted
1 C diced cooked ham
1 C dairy-free cheese chunks
½ C chopped broccoli
3 large eggs
½ C soy milk
1 tsp Lawry's seasoned salt
¼ tsp pepper

Grease bottom and sides of 9" pie pan. Preheat oven to 350 degrees.

Thaw frozen hash browns between layers of paper towel to remove excess moisture. Press potatoes into bottom of pie pan.

Drizzle melted margarine over potatoes. Bake for 25 minutes, or until lightly browned. Remove from oven and cool for 10 minutes.

In medium bowl combine ham, cheese chunks and broccoli. Spoon into potato crust.

In small bowl combine eggs, soy milk, salt and pepper. Whisk until blended. Pour egg mixture over ham mixture.

Bake for 25 – 30 minutes or until eggs are set. Let stand 5 minutes before serving.

Pumpkin Muffin Tops

Makes 36 - 48 muffin tops

1 C brown rice flour
½ C tapioca flour
½ C potato starch flour
1 C granulated sugar
1½ tsp xanthan gum
1 tsp GF baking soda
1 tsp GF allspice
2 tsp GF cinnamon
¼ tsp GF ground cloves
1 C pureed pumpkin
½ C GF applesauce
1 tsp GF vanilla

Heat oven to 350 degrees.

In large bowl cream together sugar, applesauce and vanilla. Stir in pumpkin and set aside.

In medium bowl combine flours, baking soda, salt, cinnamon, allspice and cloves.

Stir dry ingredients into pumpkin mixture, mixing well.

Drop a large spoonful onto ungreased cookie sheet. Bake for 15 – 20 minutes until browned around the edges.

Remove from cookie sheet and cool.

Fluffy Pancakes

Serves 4

1/4 C rice flour
1/2 C tapioca flour
1/4 C potato starch flour
1 tsp xanthan gum
1 tsp baking powder
2 tsp GF vanilla
2 eggs
2 Tbl vegetable oil
1 C soy milk
1 tsp cinnamon

Heat griddle or large frying pan over medium heat. Pour 2 Tbl oil into pan.

In medium bowl combine all ingredients and use wire whisk to mix until well blended.

Pour 1/4 cup batter onto hot griddle. Cook for about 3 minutes, until bubbles begin to form and bottom is brown. Flip pancake over and cook another 3 minutes until second side is brown.

Suggestion

Serve with pure maple syrup

Serve with fresh berries

Add 1/2 cup carob chips to batter
before cooking

Add 1/2 cup fresh blueberries to batter before cooking

Potato Pancakes

Serves 4

3 large potatoes
(peeled & shredded)
1 small onion, chopped
2 eggs
3 Tbl tapioca flour
½ tsp salt
¼ tsp pepper
3 Tbl vegetable oil

Place shredded potatoes in large bowl.

In small bowl beat eggs until thoroughly mixed. Add eggs to potatoes and stir to combine. Add flour, onion, salt and pepper to potatoes. Stir to combine.

Heat oil in large skillet. Place large tablespoons of potato mixture in pan. Flatten with back of spoon. Cook until bottom is brown, about
3 – 4 minutes. Using spatula, flip pancake and cook second side until brown.

Serve with GF tofu sour cream or applesauce.

Sometimes it's the smallest decisions that can change your life forever.

Keri Russell

Apple Cakes

Serves 4

1 ripe banana
2 eggs
2 Tbl vegetable oil
2 Tbl GF maple syrup
1 C soy milk
1 C tapioca flour
½ C soy flour
½ C potato starch flour
1 tsp xanthan gum
1 Tbl GF baking powder
½ tsp salt
2 C grated apple, no peelings
2 tsp GF cinnamon
¼ tsp GF nutmeg

In large bowl mix banana and eggs. Add oil, syrup and soy milk. Mix until well blended.

In medium bowl, combine flours, baking powder, salt, cinnamon and nutmeg. Add to banana mixture. Mix well.

Stir in apples. Stir until apples are well incorporated.

Heat oil on griddle or large frying pan. Drop spoonfuls onto hot pan forming circle about 3" across. (An ice cream scoop works great for this.)

Heat cakes over medium heat until bubbles appear. Flip cake and cook second side until cooked through and brown around the edges.

Serve with GF maple syrup or GF fruit preserves.

Sunshine Muffins

Serves 4

½ C brown rice flour
¾ C tapioca flour
½ C potato starch flour
1 C dried cranberries
½ tsp GF baking soda
½ tsp GF baking powder
½ tsp salt
½ tsp GF cinnamon
½ tsp GF ground cloves
2 C GF applesauce
½ C pecan pieces
1 egg
1 C GF brown sugar
½ C GF, DF margarine, softened
1 ½ tsp xanthan gum

Preheat oven to 350 degrees.

In large bowl combine flours, sugar, baking soda, baking powder, salt, cinnamon and cloves. Stir to combine.

Add cranberries, nuts, egg and applesauce. Stir until combined.

Spoon into paper lined muffin tin to ¾ full.

Bake 25 – 30 minutes or until knife inserted in center comes out clean.

Fresh Fruit with Honey Glaze

Serves 2

1 C fresh strawberries, sliced
½ C fresh raspberries
½ C fresh blackberries
1 banana, sliced
½ C honey
½ tsp GF vanilla

Combine banana, raspberries, blackberries and strawberries in medium sized bowl.

In small bowl combine honey and GF vanilla, stirring until combined.

Drizzle honey mixture over fresh fruit. Stir gently to coat fruit with honey mixture. Serve immediately.

Suggestion

Add or replace with any of the following fruits:

Blueberries
Peaches
Nectarines
Pineapple
Sliced apple
Mango slices
Papaya slices

French Toast

Serves 2

4 slices GF bread
2 eggs
½ cup soy milk
½ tsp GF cinnamon
2 Tbl GF, DF margarine

Preheat oven to 200 degrees.

In bowl large enough to place one slice of bread, mix eggs, soy milk and cinnamon. Whip with wire whisk or fork until combined.

Heat small frying pan on medium heat. Add GF margarine and stir to coat bottom of pan.

Place 1 slice of bread in egg mixture, coating bread. Turn bread over and coat second side. Place egg bread in heated pan. Cook 3 minutes or until bottom side is browned. Turn bread over and cook second side 3 minutes, or until browned. Remove from pan and place on oven-safe plate. Place plate in preheated oven to keep warm. Cook remaining slices of bread and place in oven when done.

Suggestion

Serve with pure maple syrup or other GF syrup

Serve with GF applesauce

Spread with peanut butter or almond butter

CHAPTER 9

Breads

Old Fashioned Potato Bread

Makes 1 loaf

1 ½ C rice flour
¾ C tapioca flour
¾ C potato starch flour
2 ½ tsp xanthan gum
1 ½ tsp salt
3 Tbl granulated sugar
1 pkg unflavored gelatin
¾ C grated raw potato (approx
1 fist sized potato)
¼ C vegetable oil
3 eggs
1 tsp vinegar
1½ C water
1 pkg dry yeast (1 ½ tsp)

Preheat oven to 350 degrees.

In small bowl, combine ½ C water, yeast and sugar. Mix and set aside until yeast foams.

In medium bowl beat eggs. Add oil, vinegar and water and mix thoroughly.

In large bowl combine flours, xanthan gum, salt, yeast and gelatin. Stir in the potato.

Pour wet ingredients into dry ingredients and combine with a wooden spoon until all dry ingredients are absorbed.

Place in a greased loaf pan, smoothing the top of the dough. Bake in a 350 degree oven for approximately 1 hour, or until top is brown and a knife inserted in the center comes out clean.

Run a knife around edge of bread pan to loosen from the pan. Remove bread from pan and place loaf on its side. After 10 minutes, turn loaf onto opposite side and cool additional 10 minutes. Place bread on bottom of loaf and cool another 15 minutes. Wrap in plastic wrap making sure edges are sealed completely.

Soft Tapioca Bread

Makes 2 loaves

2 C rice flour
1 ½ C tapioca flour
¼ C granulated sugar
2 ½ tsp xanthan gum
¼ C cornstarch
½ tsp salt
1 pkg dry yeast
½ cup warm water
2 tsp sugar
¼ C margarine
1 ¼ C hot water
1 tsp vinegar
2 eggs
¼ C vegetable oil

In large bowl combine flours, cornstarch, sugar, xanthan gum, and salt. In small bowl, combine warm water and 2 tsp sugar. Stir until sugar is dissolved. Sprinkle yeast on top of water, stirring to combine. Let mixture sit for 10 minutes until yeast starts to foam. Pour oil, hot water and vinegar into dry ingredients and blend on low. Add eggs and beat a few seconds. Add dissolved yeast mixture. Beat at highest speed for 4 minutes.

Spoon dough into prepared pans. Smooth top of dough with rubber spatula moistened with water. (If you leave peaks in the dough, your bread will have peaks when baked.) Let dough rise until doubled in bulk – about 50 – 60 minutes.

Bake for 50 to 60 minutes. If top is browning too fast, place a sheet of aluminum foil over the top, but do not seal edges.

Grease two 8 ½" x 4 ½" loaf pans and dust with rice flour.

Preheat oven to 350 degrees.

When bread is done, remove from pan and cool on side.

Gingerbread

Serves 4

½ C light or dark bean flour
½ C cornstarch
¼ C tapioca flour
1 tsp baking soda
1 tsp GF cinnamon
½ tsp GF ginger
½ tsp GF nutmeg
¼ tsp xanthan gum
½ C granulated sugar
¼ C honey
4 Tbl vegetable oil
½ C boiling water
2 eggs

Preheat oven to 350 degrees. Grease an 8" square cake pan with vegetable oil. Sprinkle 1/4 cup sugar in pan, tipping pan to coat bottom & sides with granulated sugar.

In medium bowl, combine flours, cornstarch, baking soda, spices and xanthan gum.

In large mixing bowl, combine 1/2 cup sugar, honey, oil, water and eggs. Stir to combine. Add flour mixture and beat well. Pour batter into prepared pan and bake 30 - 40 minutes, or until a knife inserted in center comes out clean.

Serve with dairy-free whipped topping.

Life is not measured by the number of breathes we take, but by the moments that take our breath away.

Anonymous

Skillet Cornbread

Serves 4

1 C rice flour
¾ C GF cornmeal
1 tsp xanthan gum
2 – 3 Tbl granulated sugar
2 ½ tsp baking powder
¾ tsp salt
1 Tbl GF, DF margarine
2 eggs, beaten
1 C soy milk
¼ C melted GF, DF margarine

Preheat oven to 400 degrees.

In large bowl, mix dry ingredients together. Set aside.

Melt 1 Tbl margarine in a 10" cast-iron skillet, or 8" round baking pan, in the oven. Swirl the butter around, coating bottom and sides of pan. Leave pan in oven while mixing cornbread batter. Pan must be hot when you pour the batter into it.

In small bowl combine the eggs, soy milk and ¼ cup melted margarine. Add to dry mixture until just combined.

Pour batter into the hot skillet or baking pan. Return pan to oven and bake for
15 – 20 minutes, or until toothpick inserted in center comes out clean.

Serve warm with margarine and honey.

Banana Nut Bread

Makes 1 loaf

1 C brown rice flour
1 C white rice flour
¼ C potato starch flour
¼ C tapioca flour
1 tsp xanthan gum
1 Tbl GF baking powder
½ tsp salt
1 egg
½ C GF, DF margarine
2/3 C honey or GF brown sugar
3 large bananas, mashed
½ C chopped walnuts

Preheat oven to 350 degrees.

Grease one 9 x 4 loaf pan, coat with granulated sugar.

In large bowl combine flours, xanthan gum, baking powder and salt. Set aside.

In medium bowl mix bananas, GF margarine, egg and honey (or brown sugar) and nuts.

Add wet ingredients to dry and stir until thoroughly combined. Spoon batter into bread pan. Bake for 40 minutes or until top starts to crack and knife inserted in center comes out clean.

Aivah's Bread

Makes 1 loaf

1 ¼ C rice flour
1 ¼ C tapioca flour
1 ¼ C potato starch flour
¼ C granulated sugar
3 tsp xanthan gum
2 pkgs unflavored gelatin
1 tsp salt
1 pkg dry yeast
½ C warm water
2 tsp granulated sugar
¼ C vegetable oil
1 ¼ C hot water
1 tsp vinegar
3 eggs

Grease 9 x 4 bread pan. Dust with rice flour. (Dusting with flour will make removing bread loaf easier.)

In small bowl dissolve yeast, 2 tsp sugar and ½ C warm water. Let sit for 10 minutes until it foams on top. Add oil and vinegar to yeast mixture. Mix on low with blender. Add eggs and mix on low again. Add gelatin, hot water, sugar and salt. Add flours 1 cup at a time, mixing on low. When thoroughly combined, add xanthan gum and mix well with wooden spoon. Batter will thicken as xanthan gum is absorbed. Let bread raise 30 minutes

Spoon dough into prepared bread pan. Bake at 350 degrees 40 – 50 minutes until lightly browned on top. Remove from oven and cool.

Life is the art of drawing without an eraser.

John W. Gardner

Cinnamon Rolls

Makes 12 large cinnamon rolls

½ C warm water
2 tsp granulated sugar
3 pkgs dry yeast
1 ½ C warm water
4 eggs
4 Tbl vegetable oil
1 tsp vinegar
2 C tapioca flour
1 ½ C rice flour
½ C potato starch flour
2/3 C powdered soy milk
4 tsp xanthan gum
1 ½ tsp salt
¼ C granulated sugar
1 C raisins (optional)
1 C GF brown sugar
1 ½ tsp GF cinnamon
½ C chopped nuts (optional)
¼ C softened GF, DF margarine

Grease large cookie sheet or 9 x 13 cake pan. Preheat oven to 375 degrees.

In a small bowl mix water, 2 tsp sugar and yeast. Set aside while you mix the rest of the ingredients. In medium bowl oil, vinegar, soy milk and eggs. In large bowl mix flours, xanthan gum, salt and 1/4 C sugar. Add yeast mixture to wet ingredients. Pour wet ingredients into dry ingredients and stir until combined. Add more flour, ¼ C at a time, until dough can be formed into a ball.

Put dough on counter heavily dusted with tapioca flour. Pat dough down, with floured hands, until about 2" high. Be sure top of dough is coated with tapioca flour and roll into a rectangle about 1" thick. Dot dough with softened GF margarine. Sprinkle with cinnamon, brown sugar, raisins and nuts.

Carefully, roll the long side of dough up into a roll. Using dental floss or thread, cut dough into sections about 1" thick. (Slide thread under rolled dough, pull up both sides, cross ends over top of dough and pull thread in opposite directions. This makes a cleaner cut than a knife and won't flatten the dough.) Place pinwheels onto greased cookie sheet. Bake for 20 minutes until tops are lightly browned.

Frost with powdered sugar frosting when still slightly warm

Powdered Sugar Frosting
2 C GF powdered sugar
3 tsp soy milk
3 tsp GF margarine

Combine powdered sugar, GF margarine and 1 tsp soy milk. Stir until combined. Add soy milk 1 tsp at a time until desired consistency.

Mashed Potato Bread

Makes 1 loaf

1 C rice flour
1 C tapioca flour
3 Tsp GF baking powder
1 tsp GF baking soda
1 tsp cream of tartar
½ tsp salt
2 Tbl GF, DF margarine
¼ C granulated sugar
6 egg yolks
6 egg whites
½ C mashed potatoes
¾ C soy milk

*** This is a good way to use
leftover mashed potatoes ***

Preheat oven to 350 degrees. Grease a 9 x 4" loaf pan. Dust with rice flour. In large bowl combine all dry ingredients. Set aside.

In medium bowl mix GF margarine and sugar on high speed until combined. Add egg yolks one at a time, mixing after each. Add mashed potatoes and mix until combined.

Add ¼ C soy milk to egg mixture and combine. Add 1/3 flour mixture and combine. Continue until soy milk and dry ingredients are all combined with egg mixture.

In medium bowl beat egg whites on high until soft peaks form. (Be sure to use clean beaters)
Fold egg whites into the other mixture using a rubber spatula.

Pour batter into pan. Smooth top of batter. Bake in center of oven for 50 – 60 minutes or until top is brown and toothpick inserted in center comes out clean.

GF Pizza Crust

Makes 1   16" crust

1 C brown rice flour
1 C tapioca flour
1 C potato starch flour
1 ½ tsp xanthan gum
2 tsp granulated sugar
¾ tsp salt
2 pkgs dry yeast
1 – 1 ½ C water, divided
2 eggs, lightly beaten
3 Tbl vegetable oil
1 tsp vinegar

GF pizza sauce or tomato sauce
Dairy free cheese

Suggested toppings:

Cooked chicken
Cooked ground beef
Cooked ground turkey
Broccoli
Spinach
Sliced mushrooms
Sliced olives
Pineapple chunks
Cooked, crumbled bacon

Preheat oven to 400 degrees. Grease two large pizza pans or cookie sheets. Sprinkle with cornmeal.

In small bowl combine dry yeast with sugar and ½ C warm water. Set aside until top is foamy.

In large bowl combine dry ingredients. Add 1 C water, eggs, oil and vinegar. Add yeast mixture and beat for 5 minutes until dough is smooth but not runny, adding more water if necessary.

Spoon dough onto prepared pans. Oil hands and press crust to edges of pans.

Prebake crust for 10 minutes. Remove from oven and top with sauce and desired ingredients.

Return to oven and bake 15 – 20 minutes until cheese is melted and crust is brown.

"Graham" Crackers

Makes 1 sheet of crackers

1 C rice flour
1 C tapioca flour
¼ C potato starch flour
½ C packed GF brown sugar
1 ¾ tsp GF cinnamon
1 tsp GF baking powder
½ tsp xanthan gum
½ tsp GF baking soda
½ tsp salt
7 Tbl GF, DF margarine
3 Tbl cold water
3 Tbl honey
1 tsp GF vanilla

In large bowl combine dry ingredients. Using your fingers work GF margarine into dry ingredients.

Add cold water, honey and vanilla. Combine with hands until dough is soft and can be formed into a ball. If dough is too dry, add more cold water 1 tsp at a time. Cover dough with plastic wrap and refrigerate for 1 hour.

Preheat oven to 325 degrees. Grease a cookie sheet and line with parchment paper.

Place dough on plastic wrap or wax paper dusted with rice flour. Place second sheet of plastic wrap on top of dough. Roll dough into rectangle (same size as cookie sheet) until 1/8" thickness. Remove top plastic wrap. Using bottom piece of plastic wrap, flip dough over onto cookie sheet. (plastic wrap will be on top). Remove plastic wrap.

Cut dough into 2 x 3" pieces and prick with fork.

Bake for 12 – 15 minutes until golden brown. Let crackers cool slightly. Run a sharp knife along cut marks to separate crackers. Cool in pan.

Crispy Corn Tortilla Chips

Serves 4

Version 1:

10 GF corn tortillas
Oil for frying
Salt

Version 2:

10 GF corn tortillas
Lawry's seasoned salt

Version 1:
Cut each tortilla into six triangular wedges.

Pour oil into heavy frying pan (cast iron works well) to ½" deep. Heat oil on medium heat. Oil is ready when a one tortilla wedge bubbles and floats when placed in the hot oil.

(If you are using a deep fryer, follow manufacturer's directions for heating oil.)

Fry tortilla triangles until golden brown. This will take 20 – 30 seconds. Using a slotted spoon, remove cooked tortilla chips from hot oil and drain on paper towels. Sprinkle chips with salt.

Version 2:
Preheat oven to 350 degrees. Cut each tortilla into six triangular wedges. Place tortilla pieces onto greased cookie sheet. Sprinkle with seasoned salt to taste.

Bake for 10 – 15 minutes or until chips are crisp.

CHAPTER 10

Main Meals

Black Bean Pumpkin Soup

Serves 4

1 16-oz can pumpkin (not pumpkin pie filling)
1 can black beans, drained
½ C onion, chopped
¼ C celery, chopped
½ C water
4 C GF chicken broth
1 tsp Lawry's seasoned salt
1 tsp GF cinnamon
¼ tsp GF cloves
½ tsp salt
¼ tsp pepper
½ soy milk
2 Tbl cornstarch

In small bowl, mix cornstarch and milk. Set aside. Combine remaining ingredients in large soup pot. Cook on medium heat 30 minutes.

Add milk/cornstarch mixture. Heat through stirring constantly until thickened.

Suggestion

Serve with GF crackers
Serve with GF cornbread

Turkey Burgers and Gravy

Serves 4

1 lb ground turkey or chicken
½ C chopped mushrooms
½ C chopped celery
¼ C chopped onion
½ C shredded carrots
2 T parsley
½ tsp pepper
½ tsp salt
1 tsp GF paprika
4 Tbl cornstarch
1 tsp Lawry's seasoned salt
½ C GF chicken broth
½ C GF vegetable protein flakes

¼ C vegetable oil
¼ C water

In large bowl, mix ingredients except oil and water. Form into patties.

In small bowl, mix water and cornstarch. Set aside.

Heat oil on medium heat. Place patties in pan. Cook, without turning, until bottoms are brown. Turn burgers over and brown other side. When patties are cooked through, remove from pan and place on plate. Turn heat to low under pan.

Turn heat to medium under pan and add chicken broth. Broth should bubble up and turn brown. Scrape bottom of pan to loosen drippings. Turn heat down to low and stir in soy milk. Add cornstarch mixture and stir until thickened. (If too thick, add more milk or broth. If too thin, add a little more cornstarch mixed in water.) Place burgers in gravy in pan. Spoon gravy over tops of burgers. Cover and heat for 5 minutes on low until burgers are heated through.

Serve with mashed potatoes and a steamed vegetable.

Turkey Wild Rice Casserole

Serves 4

½ C wild rice
½ C white rice
2 C cooked turkey
2 C GF chicken broth
2½ C water
2 tsp GF cornstarch
3 Tbl onion, finely chopped
½ C celery, chopped
1 tsp Lawry's seasoned salt
1 tsp GF dried basil
½ tsp pepper

Preheat oven to 350 degrees.

Cut cooked turkey into ½ inch pieces.

Mix cornstarch in 1 C water.

Combine all ingredients in 2 qt casserole pan. Cover with aluminum foil.

Cover and bake 50 - 60 minutes. Let casserole sit for 10 minutes before serving.

When we long for a life without difficulties, we need to remember that oaks grow strong in contrary winds and diamonds are made under pressure.

Peter Marshall

GF Pizza

Makes 1 - 16" crust

1 C brown rice flour
1 C tapioca flour
1 C potato starch flour
1 ½ tsp xanthan gum
2 tsp granulated sugar
¾ tsp salt
2 pkgs dry yeast
1 – 1 ½ C water, divided
2 eggs, lightly beaten
3 Tbl vegetable oil
1 tsp apple cider vinegar

GF pizza sauce or tomato sauce
Dairy-free cheese

Suggested toppings:

Cooked chicken
Cooked ground beef
Cooked ground turkey
Broccoli
Spinach
Sliced mushrooms
Sliced olives
Pineapple chunks
Cooked, crumbled bacon

Preheat oven to 400 degrees. Grease two large pizza pans or cookie sheets. Sprinkle with cornmeal.

In small bowl combine dry yeast with sugar and ½ C warm water. Set aside until top is foamy.

In large bowl combine dry ingredients. Add 1 C water, eggs, oil and vinegar. Add yeast mixture and beat for 5 minutes until dough is smooth but not runny, adding more water if necessary.

Spoon dough onto prepared pans. Oil hands and press crust to edges of pans.

Prebake crust for 10 minutes. Remove from oven and top with sauce and desired ingredients.

Return to oven and bake 15 – 20 minutes until cheese is melted and crust is brown.

Tender Beef Roast

Serves 4

3 lb beef roast
4 large potatoes, quartered
2 carrots, peeled and cut into
   chunks
1 small onion, quartered
2 tsp Lawry's seasoned salt
½ tsp pepper
½ tsp GF dried basil
½ C GF chicken broth (or water)

Preheat oven to 350 degrees.

Place roast in small roasting pan. Place potatoes, onions and carrots around roast. Sprinkle roast and vegetables with seasoned salt, pepper and basil. Pour chicken broth (or water) into bottom of pan.

Cook roast in oven for 1-1/2 hours. Baste roast and vegetables every half hour.

Let roast sit in pan for 5 minutes before removing.

Pork Chops with Mushrooms & Onions

Serves 4

4 bone-in pork chops
1 C mushrooms, sliced
1 small onion, thinly sliced
¼ C celery, chopped
1 tsp Lawry's seasoned salt
¼ tsp pepper
1 tsp GF dried basil
2 Tbl vegetable oil

Heat oil in large skillet.

While skillet is heating, coat both sides of each pork chops with salt, pepper and basil

When pan is hot, place chops in pan and cook until bottom is brown. Turn chops over. Add onions, celery and mushrooms. Stir mushrooms, onions & celery occasionally. Cook until bottom of chop is brown and onions and mushrooms are tender.

Being happy doesn't mean that everything is perfect. It means that you've decided to look beyond the imperfections.

Anonymous

Crockpot BBQ Ribs

Serves 4

8 beef or pork ribs
1-16 oz bottle GF BBQ sauce
¼ C chopped onions
¼ C chopped celery
¼ C chopped carrots
1 tsp GF dried basil
1 C water

In small bowl combine BBQ sauce, water and basil. Stir to combine.

Place ribs in crock pot. Place onion, celery & carrots over ribs. Pour BBQ sauce mixture over ribs, making sure to coat all ribs.

Put cover on crock pot and turn to low. Cook 6 – 8 hours until tender.

Serve with mashed potatoes.

** I put the ribs in the crockpot before I go to work and have dinner ready and waiting when I get home.

Southwest Shredded Pork

Serves 8

2 lbs boneless pork roast
1 C GF chicken broth
½ C GF chunky salsa
2 lg onions, quartered
1 sm green pepper, chopped
2 small garlic cloves, crushed
2 tsp GF ground cumin

Place pork roast in crockpot. Add remaining ingredients.

Cover and cook on high heat 4 – 5 hours. (Can be cooked on medium heat 6 – 8 hours.)

Remove meat from crockpot and place on plate or cutting board. Using two forks, shred meat.

Suggestion

Use shredded pork for filling in tacos, enchiladas, sandwiches.

Use turkey breast or small beef roast in place of pork.

Stuffed Mushrooms

Serves 8

1½ lb medium mushrooms
½ lb ground turkey (or beef)
2 Tbl vegetable oil
½ C dairy-free cheese
¼ C GF bread crumbs
¼ C finely chopped onion
¼ tsp GF garlic powder
½ tsp GF dried basil
½ tsp Lawry's seasoned salt

Preheat oven to 350 degrees.

Remove mushroom stems and chop finely.

Add oil to large skillet. Cook ground turkey, onion, mushroom stems and seasonings. Cook over medium heat until turkey is cooked through, stirring occasionally.

Remove from heat and stir in dairy-free cheese. Stir until cheese is melted and mixture in combined.

Fill mushroom caps with turkey mixture. Place caps on greased cookie sheet. Bake in oven for 15 minutes.

Serve immediately.

If you only do what you know you can do – you never do very much.

Tom Krause

Coconut Chicken

Serves 8

2 boneless, skinless chicken breasts
1 -13.5 oz can coconut milk
½ tsp GF seasoned salt
1/8 tsp GF red chili paste
2 Tbl finely chopped onion
1 clove garlic, crushed
4 C hot cooked white rice
2 Tbl vegetable oil

Cut chicken into 1" pieces. Sprinkle seasoned salt on chicken.

Place oil in large, deep skillet. Heat on medium heat. Cook chicken pieces 10 – 12 minutes, stirring occasionally, until chicken is cooked completely and no longer pink.

Add onions and garlic. Cook for 5 minutes until onions become transparent, stirring occasionally. Remove garlic.

Pour coconut milk over chicken mixture. Cook for 10 minutes on medium heat until sauce begins to bubble. Remove from heat.

Spoon chicken and coconut milk over hot, cooked rice.

** 1/8 tsp red chili paste is just enough to give the coconut milk flavor. If you prefer a spicier mixture, increase red chili paste to ¼ or ½ tsp **

In medium bowl mix coconut milk and red chili paste with wire whip.

Stuffed Green Peppers

Serves 4

4 green peppers
½ lb ground turkey (or beef)
2 C cooked white or brown rice
¼ C chopped onion
¼ C chopped celery
¼ C shredded carrot
1 tsp Lawry's seasoned salt
¼ tsp pepper
½ tsp GF dried basil
½ C GF chicken broth
2 Tbl oil
½ C water

Preheat oven to 350 degrees.

Grease an 8″ x 8″ square casserole pan. Add water and set aside.

Cut tops off green peppers and clean out seeds. Place peppers in casserole pan. (If peppers tip over, cut bottoms flat being careful not to cut through bottom of pepper.)

In large skillet, brown ground turkey (or beef) in oil for 10 minutes. Add onion, celery, carrot and spices and cook for an additional 10 minutes. Add broth and cooked rice. Stir to combine.

Fill peppers with filling and place in casserole pan. Cover pan and bake for 30 minutes or until peppers are tender.

Turkey Tacos

Serves 4

1 lb ground turkey
½ C GF chunky salsa
1 small onion, chopped
¼ C celery, chopped
8 GF tortilla shells
1 tsp GF dried basil
¼ tsp GF ground cumin

In large skillet brown ground turkey, onions, celery, basil and cumin. Cook, stirring occasionally until turkey is cooked completely. Add salsa and stir to combine. I

Spoon 2-3 Tbl turkey mixture onto center of tortilla. Top with desired toppings.

Fold 1" of bottom of taco over filling. Fold in each side, overlapping sides.

Toppings:

1 C chopped Roma tomatoes
1 C shredded lettuce
1 C vegan dairy free cheese, cubed
1 C dairy free tofu sour cream
GF Chunky Salsa or picante sauce

Dairy-Free Macaroni & Cheese

Serves 4

2 C cooked GF elbow pasta
1 C vegan dairy-free cheese
¼ C soy milk
½ tsp Lawry's seasoned salt
½ tsp GF dried basil

Cook the pasta according to manufacturer's directions. Drain and set aside.

In large saucepan combine remaining ingredients. Cook on low heat until cheese melts, stirring constantly. Add pasta to saucepan and stir until thoroughly combined.

** The best brand of cheese for good mac & cheese is Vegan Gourmet – Dairy Alternative - it's great because **It Melts!** You can use a combination of cheddar and mozzarella, if desired. **

They may forget what you said, but they will never forget how you made them feel.

Carl Buechner

Chef Salad

Serves 4

1 head Iceberg lettuce
4 Roma tomatoes, diced
1 carrot, shredded
2 stalks celery, sliced
½ C red onion slices
½ C walnut pieces
½ C sliced cooked turkey
GF salad dressing

Remove heart from head of lettuce. Cut into quarters. Slice each quarter into thin strips. Arrange lettuce on 4 plates.

Top lettuce with 1/4 each additional ingredients. Drizzle with GF dressing.

Salad dressing recipes can be found in the "Vegetables & Sides" section.

Chicken Fajitas

Serves 4

2 Tbl vegetable oil
1 green pepper, thin strips
1 red pepper, thin strips
1 yellow pepper, thin strips
1 large onion, sliced thin
1 large garlic clove, chopped
2 boneless, skinless chicken breasts
¼ C GF chicken broth
1 Tbl Lawry's seasoned salt
¼ tsp salt
¼ tsp pepper
½ tsp GF dried basil
½ C GF chunky salsa
½ C diced tomatoes
½ C vegan dairy-free cheese
½ C tofu sour cream
4-6 GF tortillas (page 85)

Cut chicken breasts into strips. In small bowl combine seasoned salt, salt, basil and pepper. Sprinkle mixture on chicken strips, coating all sides. Heat oil in large fry pan or wok on medium high heat. Cook chicken strips, turning occasionally until cooked through. Add onions, garlic and peppers.

Cook 10 minutes until peppers are tender. Add chicken broth and salsa. Cook 10 minutes until heated through.

Serve on GF tortillas with tomatoes, dairy-free cheese and tofu sour cream.

Chicken Noodle Casserole

Serves 6

1 batch homemade GF Pasta
  (page 86)
2 C cooked chicken pieces
1 C thinly sliced carrots
¼ C onion, chopped
½ C celery, chopped
½ tsp GF dried basil
1 tsp salt
½ tsp pepper
1 tsp GF dried parsley
3 C GF chicken broth
¼ C cornstarch

In medium saucepan, combine broth, carrots, onions, celery and spices. Cook 15 minutes until vegetables are tender. Add cornstarch and cook 5 minutes until thickened. Remove from heat.

Pre-cook pasta in boiling water. Drain and set aside

Place pre-boiled noodles in large, oven-safe casserole pan. Sprinkle chicken pieces over noodles. Pour thickened broth with vegetables over noodles. Stir to combine.

Cover and bake at 350 degrees for 30 minutes.

Chicken Salad

Serves 4

2 C cooked chicken, diced
½ C celery, chopped
¼ C onion, chopped
½ C dried cranberries
1 C grapes, halved (optional)
¼ C carrots, shredded
½ C mayonnaise
4 Tbl soy milk
¼ tsp GF dried basil
1 tsp Lawry's seasoned salt
¼ tsp pepper
2 C shredded lettuce
4 Roma tomatoes, quartered

In small bowl combine mayonnaise, milk, seasoned salt, pepper and basil. Set aside.

In large bowl combine remaining ingredients. Pour mayonnaise mixture over contents. Stir to combine.

Suggestion

Place scoop of chicken salad on 2 -3 lettuce leaves on plate.

Omit grapes, spread chicken salad on bread

Serve over tomato quarters.

Homemade Chicken Soup
with GF Noodles

Serves 8   (Makes 6 quarts of soup)

1 whole chicken
1 C celery, chopped
½ C onion, chopped
1-½ C carrots, sliced
1 large or 2 small cloves garlic, halved
2 Tbl Lawry's seasoned salt
1 tsp salt
½ tsp pepper
4 C GF chicken broth
2 C GF vegetable broth
4 C water
1 tsp GF dried basil
2 Tbl GF dried parsley

Place all ingredients in 6 quart cooking pot. Bring to boil. Turn heat down to medium and cook, covered for 2 hours. Remove chicken from pot and de-skin and de-bone. Return half the chicken to pot. Save remaining chicken for future meals (such as Chicken Salad on page 81). Continue to cook, uncovered while making noodles.

Gluten Free Noodles
½ cup tapioca flour
3 Tbl potato starch flour
1/3 cup cornstarch
½ tsp salt
1 Tbl xanthan gum
2 large eggs
1 Tbl oil

Combine dry ingredients in medium bowl. In small bowl, whisk together eggs and oil. Pour egg mixture into flour mixture and stir with fork to combine. Dough will be thick and stiff.

Dust GF bread board with cornstarch. Knead dough (adding more cornstarch as needed) until dough is firm and no longer sticky. Cut dough into quarters. Roll first section of dough to 1/8" thick. Slice dough into strips.

Drop noodles into boiling, salted water to which 1 Tbl oil has been added. Cook for 5 - 10 minutes, depending on thickness of noodles. Remove noodles with slotted spoon and drain in colander. Rinse with cold water and add to soup pot.

Roll, slice and boil remaining noodles. Add to soup.

Pork Lettuce Wraps

Serves 8

2 C cooked, shredded pork
¼ C GF chicken broth
3 Tbl apple cider vinegar
2 Tbl GF soy sauce
2 tsp vegetable oil
½ C chopped green onion
¼ C shredded carrots
1 C cooked rice
8 – 10 chilled lettuce leaves

In medium saucepan combined pork, vinegar, soy sauce, sesame oil, onions, carrots and rice. Mix well. Heat on low for 5 minutes until heated through.

Spoon 2 large spoonfuls of filling into lettuce leaf. Roll and eat.

Don't be pushed by your problems. Be led by your dreams.

Anonymous

Chicken Strips

Serves 4

2 Tbl vegetable oil
2 boneless, skinless chicken
    breasts
1 Tbl Lawry's seasoned salt
½ tsp GF dried basil
¼ tsp pepper
½ C GF chicken broth

Cut chicken breasts lengthwise into strips.

In small bowl mix seasoned salt, pepper and basil. Sprinkle on chicken strips.

Heat oil in pan. Cook chicken strips on medium heat, turning occasionally until cooked through and slightly brown. Add broth to hot pan. Continue to cook on medium heat until broth browns and coats chicken pieces. Cook until broth is gone. Chicken should be coated and brown.

Gluten Free Flour Tortillas

Makes 8 tortillas

1 C tapioca starch flour
½ C brown rice flour
½ C potato starch flour
1-½ tsp xanthan gum
2 tsp granulated sugar
1 tsp salt
1 C warm water
1 Tbl vegetable oil

In medium bowl, combine dry ingredients. Add water and oil, stirring to combine until dough can be formed into a ball. (Fingers work the best for mixing.) Add more tapioca starch flour if necessary.

Separate dough into 8-12 pieces and roll each piece into a ball. Place all but one of the dough balls back into the bowl and cover with plastic wrap until you're ready to work with them.

Sprinkle a clean, flat surface with a bit of tapioca flour and roll ball into a round shape. Get as thin as possible.

Heat oil on griddle or large frying pan. Cook tortilla about 1 minute or until it starts puffing up and the bottom starts to brown. Flip the tortilla and cook other side until it starts to brown.

Remove tortilla and place on waiting plate. Repeat rolling and cooking the remaining 7 tortillas. Rolling out the next tortilla while the previous tortilla is cooking works best.

Gluten Free Pasta

Makes 2 cups pasta

½ C tapioca flour
3 Tbl potato starch flour
1/3 C cornstarch
½ tsp salt
1 Tbl xanthan gum
2 large eggs
1 Tbl vegetable oil

Combine dry ingredients in medium bowl.

In small bowl, whisk together eggs. Pour egg mixture into flour mixture and stir with fork to combine. Dough will be thick and stiff.

Dust GF bread board with cornstarch. Knead dough (adding more cornstarch as needed) until dough is firm and no longer sticky. Cut dough into quarters. Roll first section of dough to 1/8" thick. Slice dough into strips.

Drop noodles into boiling, salted water to which 1 Tbl oil has been added. Cook for 5 - 10 minutes, depending on thickness of noodles. Remove noodles with slotted spoon and drain in colander. Rinse with cold water and add to soup pot. Roll, slice and boil remaining noodles and add to soup.

Marinara Sauce

Serves 4

2 large garlic cloves, minced
1-½ C water
1-½ C tomato sauce
1 six ounce can tomato paste
1 tsp GF dried basil
½ C onion, chopped
1 Tbl vegetable oil
1 bay leaf
1 tsp GF oregano

In medium saucepan, heat oil over medium heat. Sauté' onions and garlic until soft, about 10 minutes. Add remaining ingredients to saucepan. Simmer, stirring occasionally for about 45 minutes. Sauce will thicken as it cooks.

Suggestion

Serve over gluten free pasta (page 86)

Use as a dipping sauce for GF bread

Obstacles are things a person sees when he takes his eyes off his goal.

E. Joseph Cossman

Erin's Red Pepper Tomato Sauce

Serves 4

2 large or 3 small red peppers
5 or 6 cloves of garlic
¼ C vegetable oil

1-28oz can whole peeled
tomatoes (in juice)
1 Tbl GF dried basil
1 Tbl GF dried rosemary
½ Tbl GF dried thyme

½ tsp salt
¼ tsp pepper

Preheat oven to 400 degrees.

Cut peppers in half. Remove seeds and membrane. Rub oil on peppers and place on greased cookie sheet.

Remove outer skin from garlic cloves. Put garlic in tinfoil. Drizzle 4 Tbl oil over garlic. Close and seal foil over garlic. Place garlic on cookie sheet with red peppers.

Roast in oven for 15 – 20 minutes until peppers are charred and garlic is golden. Remove cookie sheet from oven.

While peppers roast, combine tomatoes with juice, olive oil and spices in large saucepan. Cook on medium heat for 15 minutes.

Once peppers are done, peel skin from peppers, chop into small pieces and add to tomato mixture. Add roasted garlic to mixture and cook for 5 minutes. Put tomato mixture into a blender, half at a time and blend until smooth.

GF Pizza

Makes 1 - 16" crust

1 C brown rice flour
1 C tapioca flour
1 C potato starch flour
1 ½ tsp xanthan gum
2 tsp granulated sugar
¾ tsp salt
2 Tbl dry yeast (2 pkgs)
1 – 1 ½ C water, divided
2 eggs, lightly beaten
3 Tbl vegetable oil
1 tsp apple cider vinegar

GF pizza sauce or tomato sauce
Dairy-free cheese
Desired ingredients

Preheat oven to 400 degrees. Grease two large pizza pans or cookie sheets. Sprinkle with cornmeal.

In small bowl combine dry yeast with sugar and ½ C warm water. Set aside until top is foamy.

In large bowl combine dry ingredients. Add 1 C water, eggs, oil and vinegar. Add yeast mixture and beat for 5 minutes until dough is smooth but not runny, adding more water if necessary.

Spoon dough onto prepared pans. Oil hands and press crust to edges of pans.

Prebake crust for 10 minutes. Remove from oven and top with sauce and desired ingredients.

Return to oven and bake 15 – 20 minutes until cheese is melted and crust is brown.

Pizza Sauce

Makes enough for 1 pizza

2 Tbl vegetable oil
2 cloves garlic, chopped fine
¼ C onion, chopped fine
1½ C tomato sauce
½ tsp GF dried oregano
1 tsp GF dried basil
½ tsp salt
¼ tsp pepper
2 Tbl cornstarch

Place oil in medium saucepan. Add onions and garlic. Cook over medium heat until tender.

Add tomato sauce and spices. Continue to cook over medium heat for 5 minutes until flavors are combined.

Add 2 Tbl cornstarch and stir until sauce has thickened.

Turkey Burgers

Serves 4 – 6

2 Tbl vegetable oil
½ lb ground turkey
½ C GF vegetable protein
flakes
¼ C GF chicken broth
½ C chopped mushrooms
¼ C chopped celery
¼ C shredded carrots
1 small clove garlic, finely
chopped
½ tsp Lawry's seasoned salt
¼ tsp pepper
½ tsp GF dried basil
1 egg

In small bowl combine vegetable protein and chicken broth. Stir to combine and set aside.

In large bowl combine remaining ingredients except oil. Add softened vegetable protein. Mix thoroughly (Mixing with hands works best.) Form into 4 - 6 patties.

Heat oil in large frying pan on medium high heat. Cook patties about 10 minutes. Flip and cook an additional 10 minutes.

Serve on buns with lettuce, tomato, onions and mayonnaise.

Turkey Chili

Serves 4

1 lb ground turkey
¼ C onion, chopped
2 Tbl vegetable oil
1 can kidney beans, not drained
1-16 oz can tomato sauce
¼ C celery, chopped
1 large clove garlic, finely
              chopped
1 Tbl Lawry's seasoned salt
½ tsp GF chili powder

In large skillet, brown ground turkey in oil. Add onion and celery. Cook 10 minutes, until onions are tender.

In large kettle, combine remaining ingredients. Add cooked turkey. Cook 20 minutes on medium heat until thickened.

Top with 1 Tbl tofu sour cream and dairy-free cheese.

Toppings:

Serve with GF cornbread

GF tofu sour cream
Shredded dairy-free cheese

Life is what you make it. Always has been. Always will be.

Grandma Moses

Turkey Meat Loaf

Serves 4

1 lb ground turkey
½ C GF vegetable protein
   flakes
¼ C GF chicken broth
½ C celery, chopped
¼ C onion, chopped
¼ C carrots, shredded
   (1 lg carrot)
1 egg
1 tsp Lawry's seasoned salt
¼ tsp pepper
½ tsp GF dried basil

In small bowl combine vegetable protein and chicken broth. Stir to combine and set aside.

In large bowl, combine remaining ingredients. (Mixing with hands works best.) Add softened vegetable protein and mix to combine. Place mixture in prepared loaf pan.

Bake at 350 degrees for 35 minutes, until cooked through. Let meatloaf sit for 5 minutes before removing from pan. Slice and serve

If a loaf pan is not available, place on greased cookie sheet and form into a loaf shape. Bake as above.

Vegetable Stir Fry

Serves 4

½ C celery, sliced
½ C carrots, julienne
½ C onion, sliced
½ C broccoli florets
½ C pea pods, sliced in half
½ C bok choy, sliced (optional)
½ C GF chicken broth
1 Tbl cornstarch
1 clove garlic, finely chopped
3 Tbl vegetable oil
1 Tbl Lawry's seasoned salt

Heat oil in large skillet or wok over medium heat. Add carrots, celery and pea pods. Cook 10 minutes until vegetables are tender. Add onions, broccoli, bok choy and garlic. Cook additional 10 minutes.

In small bowl combine GF chicken broth, seasoned salt and cornstarch. Pour mixture over vegetables in pan, stirring until sauce thickens.

Serve over hot rice or GF spaghetti noodles.

Suggestion

1 C cooked chicken can be added with carrots, if desired.

Peanut Butter Surprise Sandwich

Serves 1

2 slices GF bread
1 Tbl GF, DF margarine
2 - 3 Tbl peanut butter

Spread GF margarine on both slices of bread. Spread peanut butter on 1 slice of bread. Add one or more of the following ingredients:

Sliced dill pickles
GF potato chips
Sliced bananas
1/4 cup carob chips
1 slice dairy free cheese
2 Tbl fruit preserve

Suggestion

Substitute almond butter for peanut butter

☺ Aivah's favorite is peanut butter and pickle ☺

Green Eggs & Ham

Serves 4

6 eggs
1 C cooked ham, cubed
¼ C soymilk
½ tsp Lawry's seasoned salt
Salt & pepper to taste
6 drops green GF food color
3 Tbl GF, DF margarine

In large bowl combine eggs and soy milk until well blended. Stir in ham, food color, seasoned salt, salt and pepper.

Heat margarine in large skillet until melted. Pour egg mixture into pan. Cook over medium heat, stirring gently until all egg mixture is cooked through.

Serve immediately.

If you can find a path with no obstacles, it probably doesn't lead anywhere.

Frank A. Clark

CHAPTER 11

Vegetables,
Salads & Sides

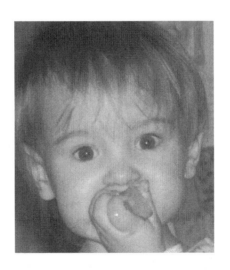

Basic White Rice

Makes 3 cups

1 C white rice
2 C water

In large saucepan combine water and rice. Cook uncovered over medium heat until water begins to boil.

I prefer Jasmine or Basmati

Reduce heat to low and cover pan. Cook for 20 minutes or until all water has been absorbed.

Serve hot or store in airtight container in refrigerator.

Suggestion

Replace 1 cup of water with 1 cup chicken stock or chicken broth to add flavor.

Basic Brown Rice

Makes 3 cups

1 C brown rice
2 C water

In large saucepan combine water and rice. Cook uncovered over medium heat until water begins to boil.

Reduce heat to low and cover pan. Cook for 30 minutes or until all water has been absorbed.

Serve hot or store in airtight container in refrigerator.

Foolproof Hardboiled Eggs

Makes 3 cups

6 eggs
Water
½ tsp salt

Place eggs in large saucepan. Cover with water and add salt.

Bring water to boil over high heat. When water begins to boil, cover and remove from heat. Let eggs stand, covered, for 20 minutes.

Pour off water and fill saucepan with cold water. Let sit for 5 minutes. Eggs are ready to use.

This process works for 1 egg or 12.

Life's challenges are not supposed to paralyze you. They're supposed to help you discover who you are.

Bernice Johnson Reagon

Basic Chicken Stock

Makes 4 qts

1 chicken, whole or cut up
1 qt GF, DF chicken broth
3 qt water
3 carrots, peeled & cut up
3 stalks celery, cut up
1 small onion, cut up
1 Tbl GF dried basil
2 tsp Lawry's seasoned salt
1 tsp salt
½ tsp pepper
½ tsp GF paprika
1 clove garlic, halved

In large soup pot combine all ingredients. Bring to a boil. Reduce heat to medium low and cook, covered, for 1 hour. Stock should bubble, but not be at a hard boil.

Remove chicken from stock and save for use in other recipes.

Continue cooking stock, uncovered, over medium heat for 1 hour. This will reduce the stock and concentrate the flavors.

Store in airtight containers in refrigerator for up to one week.

Stock can be frozen in airtight, freezer proof containers.

I freeze the stock in ice cube trays, then store the stock "cubes" in freezer-proof plastic bags. This is great when you want to add a little chicken flavor to foods.

Refrigerator Pickles

Makes 4 cups

4 C thinly sliced cucumbers
1 large onion, thinly sliced
1 C apple cider vinegar
1 C granulated sugar
¾ C hot water
½ tsp GF pickling spice

In large bowl, combine cucumbers and onions. Set aside. In medium bowl, combine sugar and hot water. Stir until sugar is dissolved. Add remaining ingredients and stir to combine. Pour mixture over cucumbers and onions, stirring until cucumbers and onions are coated with liquid. Cover and refrigerate.

Pickles will be ready to eat in 24 hours.

Suggestion

Add or substitute one or more of the following vegetables:

Broccoli florets
Cauliflower pieces
Thinly sliced carrots
Fresh green beans
Sugar snap peas

Sweet & Sour Salad Dressing

Makes 2 cups

2 C granulated sugar
1/3 C vegetable oil
1 C apple cider vinegar
1 tsp GF dried parsley
1 tsp GF dried oregano
1 tsp GF onion powder
½ tsp GF garlic powder
¼ tsp salt
1/8 tsp pepper

Place all ingredients in large, covered container with a tight sealing lid. Shake until combined.

Refrigerate for ½ hour. Shake to combine right before serving.

Serve over tossed salad.

Oriental Salad Dressing

Makes 1-¼ cup

½ C apple cider vinegar
¼ C water
¼ C GF soy sauce
2 Tbl water
1 tsp GF sesame oil
¼ C vegetable oil

In covered container with airtight lid, combine all ingredients. Shake well.

Shake right before serving.

Life is 10% what happens to you and 90% how you react to it

Charles R. Swindoll

Raspberry Vinaigrette

Makes 1 cup

1 pint fresh raspberries
¼ C apple cider vinegar

¾ tsp GF dried basil
¼ tsp GF thyme
½ tsp salt
¼ tsp pepper
½ tsp granulated sugar

¼ C olive or vegetable oil

Puree raspberries in blender or food processor. Place pureed raspberries in large bowl.

Add vinegar and mix with wire whisk.

Add spices and whisk to combine.

While whisking, pour thin, steady stream of oil into mixture until thoroughly combined.

Store in airtight container in refrigerator until ready to use.

** This does not keep long in the refrigerator and should be made the same day you plan to use it **

French Dressing

Makes 1½ cup

¼ C granulated sugar
3 Tbl water
1 C vegetable
½ C GF ketchup
3 tsp apple cider vinegar
½ tsp GF celery salt
½ tsp GF paprika
½ tsp Lawry's seasoned salt
1 Tbl GF Worcestershire sauce
¼ C finely chopped onion

In small saucepan combine water and sugar. Cook over low heat, stirring constantly, until sugar is dissolved and syrup is thick. Remove from heat and cool syrup.

Add remaining ingredients to sugar syrup and whisk until well blended.

Store in refrigerator until ready to use.

Life is a great big canvas and you should throw all the paint you can on it.

Danny Kaye

Deviled Eggs

Serves 6

6 hard boiled eggs
½ C GF mayonnaise
2 T finely chopped onion
1 tsp Lawry's seasoned salt
½ tsp salt
¼ tsp pepper
½ tsp GF dried basil
GF paprika

Cut eggs in half lengthwise. Gently remove yolks, being careful not to break whites.

In medium bowl mash egg yolks with fork. Add onion and seasonings to egg yolks, stirring to combine. Add mayonnaise and stir until smooth.

Spoon egg yolk mixture into egg white halves. Sprinkle with paprika.

Refrigerate until ready to eat.

Roasted Potatoes

Serves 4

8 small white or red potatoes
¼ C vegetable oil
1 tsp salt
½ tsp pepper
1 tsp Lawry's seasoned salt
2 cloves garlic, minced

Preheat oven to 350 degrees.

Cut potatoes into quarters and place in large bowl. Pour oil over potatoes and gently toss so all pieces are coated with oil.

Sprinkle remaining ingredients over potatoes and gently toss to distribute spices and garlic.

Place potatoes on ungreased cookie sheet and spread out evenly.

Roast for 30 – 45 minutes until browned. Flip potatoes 2 – 3 times during baking period to ensure even roasting.

Apple Butter

Serves 8

1 qt GF applesauce
1½ C granulated sugar
3 tsp GF cinnamon
½ tsp GF allspice
¼ tsp GF ground cloves

In large saucepan combine all ingredients. Heat on high to boil. Boil for 10 minutes. Reduce heat to medium and simmer for 30 minutes.

Store in airtight container in refrigerator.

Spread apple butter on GF bread or GF crackers.

Apple butter is a wonderful filling between layers of GF cake.

Potato Salad

Serves 4

4 C potatoes, boiled and cubed
2 hard boiled eggs, diced
½ C celery, chopped
¼ C onion, chopped
1 Tbl Lawry's seasoned salt
½ tsp pepper
½ C mayonnaise
4 Tbl soy milk
¼ tsp GF dried basil

In small bowl, combine mayonnaise, soy milk, seasoned salt, pepper and basil. Set aside.

In large bowl, combine potatoes, eggs, celery and onions. Pour mayonnaise mixture over all and stir gently to combine.

Refrigerate for 1 hour before serving.

Creamed Potatoes with Fresh Parsley

Serves 4

4 large potatoes, peeled and
  cubed
1 C soy milk
2 Tbl GF margarine
2 Tbl cornstarch
1 Tbl fresh parsley, chopped
  fine
½ tsp salt
¼ tsp pepper

Boil potatoes until soft. Drain and set aside.

In large saucepan melt margarine. Add remaining ingredients, stirring to combine. Heat on low, stirring constantly, until mixture thickens. Add drained potatoes to sauce. Stir gently to coat potatoes. Heat 2 – 3 minutes until potatoes are heated through.

Without mistakes we lose the chance to learn

Anonymous

Old Fashioned Hash Browns

Serves 4

6 small or 3 large potatoes, diced
¼ C celery, chopped
¼ C onion, chopped
1 tsp Lawry's seasoned salt
¼ tsp pepper
¼ C vegetable oil

In large frying pan heat oil on medium heat. Add potatoes and cook until potatoes are tender and slightly browned, about 15 minutes.

Add remaining ingredients. Cook and additional 10 – 15 minutes until potatoes are browned.

Serve immediately.

Garlic Mashed Potatoes

Serves 4

4 large, unpeeled potatoes
1 small clove garlic, finely
  chopped
½ C soy milk
4 Tbl GF, DF margarine
½ tsp Lawry's seasoned salt
¼ tsp pepper

Cut potatoes into 6 - 8 pieces each. Boil in salted water until soft, about 20 minutes. Drain potatoes. Put potatoes back into pan and add remaining ingredients. Whip with electric mixer until smooth.

Suggestion

Stir in 1 cup steamed broccoli florets after potatoes are whipped.

Home Fried Potatoes

Serves 4

3 C potatoes, sliced
¼ C onion, chopped
1 clove garlic, finely chopped
¼ C celery, finely chopped
3 Tbl vegetable oil
1 Tbl Lawry's seasoned salt
1 tsp GF paprika
¼ tsp pepper

In large frying pan, heat oil over medium heat. Add potatoes and celery. Sprinkle with seasoned salt, pepper and paprika.

Cook until potatoes are tender and slightly browned, about 15 minutes. Stir potatoes occasionally to avoid sticking to pan.

Add remaining ingredients and cook an additional 10 minutes. Serve immediately

Life is like a piano . . . what you get out of it depends on how you play it.

Anonymous

Caramel Fruit Dip

Serves 4 – 6

8 oz tofu cream cheese
1 C GF brown sugar
Apple slices
Banana slices

In medium saucepan heat cream cheese until just melted. Remove from heat and add brown sugar. Beat on high until completely mixed.

Serve over apple and banana slices.

Refrigerate remaining caramel dip.

Dill Dip

Serves 4 – 6

1 C mayonnaise
¼ C finely chopped onion
1 C tofu sour cream
1 Tbl GF dried parsley
1 Tbl GF dill weed
1 tsp Lawry's seasoned salt

Celery sticks
Carrot sticks

In medium bowl combine tofu sour cream and mayonnaise. Add remaining ingredients and stir until thoroughly combined.

Serve with celery and carrot sticks.

Stuffed Celery

Makes 2 dozen

1–12 oz pkg tofu sour cream
24 – 6″ long pieces of celery
¼ C chopped pecans
½ C dried cranberries

Fill hollows of each piece of celery with tofu sour cream. Sprinkle with chopped pecans. Place 6 – 8 dried cranberries along each piece of celery.

Suggestion

Use GF peanut butter instead of tofu sour cream.

We are all blessed with great opportunities disguised as impossible situations.

Anonymous

Rosemary Potatoes

Serves 4

6 medium red potatoes
1 Tbl fresh rosemary, chopped
2 Tbl finely chopped onion
½ tsp GF dried basil
1 tsp salt
¼ tsp pepper
3 Tbl vegetable oil

Cut potatoes into 6 – 8 pieces each, leaving skins on. Place potato pieces in medium saucepan. Cover potatoes with water. Cook over medium heat until water boils. Continue to boil until potato pieces are tender – about 20 – 30 minutes.

While potatoes cook, place oil in large frying pan. Heat over low heat until melted. Add onion and cook until onions are translucent.

Add drained potatoes to frying pan and cook for 5 – 10 minutes until potatoes start to brown. Add rosemary, basil, salt and pepper. Cook for an additional 5 minutes.

Serve immediately.

Easy Fruit Salad

Serves 4

3 apples, cored & sliced
1-15 oz can mandarin oranges
2 C green or red grapes
1 pt fresh strawberries
½ C walnuts, chopped
1-15 oz can pineapple chunks
3 C dairy-free whipped topping

Drain mandarin oranges. Drain pineapple chunks. Save juice from mandarin oranges and pineapple. Cut strawberries in half.

In large bowl, combine fruits and walnuts. Add whipped topping and stir gently until fruit is covered with whipped topping.

Refrigerate 1 hour before serving.

Suggestion

Combine juice from mandarin oranges and pineapple with 1 C sparkling water or GF lemon-lime soda for a fruity sparkling drink.

Creamy Cole Slaw

Serves 4

1 small head cabbage, shredded
¼ C onion, chopped fine
¼ C carrots, peeled & shredded
¾ C mayonnaise
3 Tbl vegetable oil
3 Tbl apple cider vinegar
½ C granulated sugar
½ tsp salt

In large bowl, combine cabbage, onion and carrots. Set aside.

In medium bowl combine remaining ingredients. Stir until combined.

Pour mayonnaise mixture over cabbage mixture. Stir gently until combined.

Refrigerate for 2 hours before serving.

Life is not the way it's supposed to be – it's the way it is. The way we cope with it is what makes the difference.

Anonymous

Sunshine Squares

Serves 4

4 pkgs unflavored gelatin
¾ C pineapple juice
1 C boiling water
¼ C granulated sugar
1 C orange juice

In large bowl soften gelatin in pineapple juice. Add boiling water and stir until dissolved. Add sugar and orange juice, stirring until sugar is dissolved.

Pour into ungreased 9" x 9" pan. Refrigerate for 2 hours until set. Cut into squares.

Squares can be left unrefrigerated up to 4 hours without melting.

Suggestions:

Any type of GF juice can be used.

Try the following, alone or combined:

Apple
Cranberry
Grape
Pineapple
Orange
White Grape
Pomegranate
Peach

Wiggly Apples

Serves 4

1 -12-oz can GF frozen apple
juice concentrate, thawed
3 pkgs unflavored gelatin
1½ C water

Grease a 13" x 9" pan with GF margarine. Put pan in refrigerator to cool.

In medium bowl, soften gelatin in apple juice.

In large saucepan bring water to a boil. Remove from heat and add to apple juice. Stir until combined.

Pour mixture into cooled pan and refrigerate 1 hour. Cut into 1" squares. Store in airtight container in refrigerator.

Very Berry Ice

Serves 2

1 pint fresh berries
(strawberries, raspberries,
blackberries or a combination)
¾ C granulated sugar
¾ C water
¼ C apple juice

Puree berries in blender.

In small saucepan heat water and sugar until sugar melts. Continue to heat over medium heat until it thickens to syrup – about 10 – 15 minutes.

Pour syrup into blender with berries. Blend until smooth and combined.

Pour into plastic container, ice cube trays or popsicle molds. Freeze until firm.

Look at everything as though you were seeing it for the first or last time.

Betty Smith

Citrus Mousse

Serves 4

1 pkgs unflavored gelatin
3 Tbl cold water
2 eggs, separated
4 Tbl granulated sugar
Juice from 1 lemon
Grated rind from ½ lemon
1-1/3 C dairy-free whipped
  topping

** Replace orange juice and rind for lemon for a different flavor **

In small saucepan sprinkle gelatin over cold water. Set aside.

In large bowl combine egg yolks and sugar. Beat at high speed until light yellow and fluffy. Add juice and rind. Stir gently to combine.

Heat gelatin over low heat until just melted. Add to egg yolk mixture and stir until just combined.

Fold whipped topping into egg yolk mixture.

In medium bowl beat egg whites until stiff peaks form. Fold egg whites into egg yolk mixture.

Spoon mousse into 4 small serving bowls. Refrigerate 2 hours before serving.

CHAPTER 12

Sweets

Whoopie Pies

Makes 2 dozen double cookies

1 egg
1/3 C vegetable oil
1 C granulated sugar
1 C tapioca starch flour
½ C rice flour
½ C potato starch flour
½ C unsweetened cocoa
1 tsp GF baking soda
¾ C soy milk
1 tsp GF vanilla
1 Tbl unflavored gelatin (1 pkg)
1-½ tsp xanthan gum

1 recipe Homemade
Marshmallows (page 148)

Preheat oven to 350 degrees. Grease two large cookie sheets and set aside.

In large bowl beat egg, sugar, gelatin and oil until pale yellow in color. Add soy milk and GF vanilla and beat until blended. Add baking soda and cocoa, beating until mixed. Add flours and cornstarch. Beat until combined. Add xanthan gum, stirring vigorously until combined and thickened. Let batter sit for 10 minutes (this gives the xanthan gum time to thicken the batter).

Drop by teaspoonfuls onto cookie sheets. Cookies will spread and flatten as they bake. Bake for 10 - 12 minutes until batter is firm and not liquid on the top. Be careful not to over bake. Remove from pan and cool on paper towels.

Let cookies cool for about 10 - 15 minutes. (If cookies are too hot, marshmallow filling will melt and make a really big mess! I know this from experience!)

Place homemade marshmallow between two slightly warm cookies. The warmth from the cookies will melt the marshmallow slightly so they stick together.

Chocolate Mayonnaise Cupcakes

Makes 20 brownies

1 C soy flour
½ C tapioca flour
½ C potato starch flour
1 pkg unflavored gelatin
1 ½ tsp xanthan gum
2/3 C unsweetened cocoa
1-2/3 C granulated sugar
1-½ tsp GF baking soda
1 tsp GF baking powder
1 C GF mayonnaise
1-1/3 C water
3 eggs

** This is a soft, moist cake.
Since soy flour is used instead of
rice flour, the texture is not
grainy **

Preheat oven to 350 degrees.

Place cupcake papers into cupcake pan (or grease & sugar cups in cupcake pan).

In large bowl combine eggs and sugar. Mix on high for 2 – 3 minutes until light and fluffy and pale yellow. Reduce to low and blend in mayonnaise.

Add 1/3 C water and the soy flour. Mix until well blended. Add another 1/3 C water and tapioca flour, mixing until blended. Mix in remaining 2/3 C water. Add potato starch flour, gelatin, baking soda, baking powder and cocoa. Mix until well blended. Mix in gelatin and xanthan gum. Mixture will thicken once the xanthan gum is added.

Fill cupcake papers 2/3 full. Bake for 20 minutes or until top springs back when pressed gently.

** This recipe will make 2 8" round cakes. Bake cakes for 30 – 35 minutes until top springs back when pressed gently.

Fudge Brownies

Makes 8 brownies

1 C water
½ C GF, DF margarine
½ C uncooked cream of rice cereal
1 egg
1 tsp GF vanilla
1 tsp GF cinnamon
1 C granulated sugar
4 Tbl unsweetened cocoa
1 tsp GF baking powder
¼ C chopped pecans (optional)

Preheat oven to 350 degrees.

Grease 8 x 8 x 2" cake pan. (Recipe can be doubled and baked in a 9 x 13" pan.)

In medium saucepan heat water & margarine to boil. Sprinkle in cereal and cook for 1 minute. Remove from heat, cover and let sit for 5 minutes.

Stir egg and vanilla into cooked cereal. Set aside.

In medium bowl combine sugar, cocoa, cinnamon and GF baking powder. Add cereal mixture and stir until combined. Stir in nuts if desired.

Spread mixture in the pan, smoothing top of mixture.

Bake for 40 – 50 minutes until toothpick inserted in center comes out clean.

Cool and cut into 2" squares.

Pumpkin Pie

Makes 1 pie

1-15 oz canned pumpkin
1 C soy milk
2 Tbl melted GF, DF margarine
2 large eggs
2 Tbl tapioca flour
½ C GF brown sugar
¼ C granulated sugar
½ tsp salt
2 tsp GF cinnamon
1-½ tsp GF nutmeg
½ tsp GF cloves

1 GF pie crust (page 146)

Preheat oven to 350 degrees.

Grease 10" pie pan.

In large bowl, mix all liquid ingredients. In medium bowl mix all dry ingredients. Slowly mix dry ingredients into wet ingredients. Beat until combined.

Pour into prepared pie shell, leafing at least ¼" between batter and top of pie crust. Smooth top of filling.

Bake for 45 minutes or until a knife inserted into pie comes out clean.

If crust gets brown too fast, cover crust only with aluminum foil.

I don't think of all the misery, but of all the beauty that still remains.

Anne Frank

White Cake

Makes 1 cake

½ C rice flour
¼ C potato starch flour
¼ C tapioca flour
¼ C cornstarch
¾ tsp xanthan gum
1 pkg unflavored gelatin
1 tsp GF baking soda
1 tsp GF baking powder
½ tsp salt
1/3 C vegetable oil
¾ C granulated sugar
1 tsp GF vanilla
1/3 C soy milk
3 eggs

Preheat oven to 350 degrees. Grease an 8-½" square or round cake pan and dust with granulated sugar.

In medium bowl mix flours, cornstarch, xanthan gum, gelatin, baking soda, baking powder and salt. Set aside.

In medium bowl, mix oil and sugar. Add eggs and vanilla and mix thoroughly. Add soy milk and combine.

Add dry ingredients and mix just to combine. Spoon batter into prepared pan. Bake 25 - 30 minutes until knife inserted in center comes out clean.

Nobody can go back and start a new beginning, but anyone can start today and make a new ending.

Maria Robinson

Moist Chocolate Cake

Makes 1 cake

1-½ C rice flour
½ C tapioca flour
¼ C potato starch flour
1-¼ tsp xanthan gum
1-¼ tsp GF baking soda
1 tsp GF baking powder
½ tsp salt
½ C GF carob chips
½ C hot water
¾ C vegetable oil
2 C granulated sugar
4 eggs
1 C soy milk
1 tsp GF vanilla

Preheat oven to 350 degrees. Grease two 9" cake pans and dust with granulated sugar.

In medium bowl mix flours, xanthan gum, baking powder, GF baking soda and salt. Set aside.

In small microwave safe bowl, combine carob chips and water. Microwave on defrost for 1-1/2 minutes or until carob chips are melted. Stir to combine. Set aside.

In large bowl mix oil and sugar. Add eggs and beat until light yellow. Pour in melted carob and mix well. Add soy milk and GF vanilla and mix well. Add dry ingredients and mix slowly until combined.

Pour into prepared pans and bake cakes 35 - 45 minutes.

Pound Cake

Makes 1 cake

1-½ C rice flour
½ C tapioca flour
¼ C potato starch flour
1-¼ tsp xanthan gum
1 tsp salt
1-¼ C granulated sugar
2/3 C GF margarine
1/2 C soy milk
3 eggs

Glaze

½ C granulated sugar
¼ C GF fruit preserves
   (any flavor)

Preheat oven to 325 degrees. Grease Bundt pan and dust with granulated sugar.

In large bowl mix flours, xanthan gum, salt and sugar. Add GF margarine and soy milk. Mix on low until combined.

Add eggs and mix about 2 minutes until fluffy. Spoon batter into prepared pan and bake for 1 hour and 10 minutes or until knife inserted in center comes out clean.

Cool in pan for 5 minutes before turning out onto plate.

Glaze instructions:

In small saucepan heat sugar and fruit preserves on low, stirring constantly. Drizzle or brush glaze on cake.

Spicy Carrot Cake

Makes 1 cake

½ C rice flour
1 C tapioca flour
½ C potato starch flour
1 tsp xanthan gum
2 tsp GF baking soda
2-½ tsp GF cinnamon
½ tsp GF ginger
¼ tsp GF cloves
½ tsp salt
4 eggs
2 C granulated sugar
1 C mayonnaise
1-16oz can crushed pineapple
3 C shredded carrots
½ C chopped walnuts
½ C raisins

Grease 9" x 13" cake pan and dust with granulated sugar.

In medium bowl, stir together flours, xanthan gum, baking soda, cinnamon, ginger, cloves and salt. Set aside.

In large bowl beat together eggs, sugar, mayonnaise and undrained pineapple. Add flour mixture and beat until well mixed. Stir in carrots, raisins and walnuts.

Pour batter into prepared pan. Bake for 45 - 50 minutes or until knife inserted in center comes out clean. Cool in pan.

When ready to serve, spread top with dairy-free whipped topping

How wonderful it is that nobody need wait a single moment before starting to improve the world.

Anne Frank

Cut-Out Cookies

Makes 3 dozen

1 C granulated sugar
1 C GF, DF margarine
1 egg
1 tsp GF vanilla
1 C rice flour
¾ C tapioca flour
½ C potato starch flour
1½ tsp xanthan gum
¼ tsp salt

½ C tapioca flour
½ C granulated sugar

Preheat oven to 350 degrees.

In large bowl combine sugar and margarine. Mix until fluffy and light yellow. Add egg and vanilla. Mix until combined.

Add salt, xanthan gum and flours, mixing until smooth. You may want to mix with hands if dough gets too thick for mixer.

Form dough into a ball, cover with plastic wrap and refrigerate one hour until firm.

Mix tapioca flour and sugar in small bowl. Sprinkle counter or cutting board with sugar/flour mixture.

Take half the cookie dough and roll out to ¼" thickness. Cut with cookie cutters. Transfer cookies to ungreased, non-stick cookie sheet.

Bake 10 – 12 minutes or until edges begin to brown. Cool cookies for 2 minutes on cookie sheet. Remove from cookie sheet and let cool completely.

Baked Alaska

Makes 1 cake

3 egg whites
4 Tbl granulated sugar
1 round GF single layer cake
½ C GF raspberry preserves
1 pt vanilla soy ice cream

½ C fresh raspberries (optional)

Preheat oven to 350.

In medium bowl beat egg whites until stiff peaks form. Fold in sugar. Set aside.

Place cake layer on oven proof plate. (If oven proof plate is not available, place on bottom of spring form pan.)

Spread preserves on top of cake, leaving ½" around edges.

Spoon soy ice cream into a mound, on top of preserves. Cover ice cream and sides of cake with beaten egg whites.

Bake in oven 5 minutes or until egg whites turn a light brown color.

Garnish with fresh raspberries if desired.

To be upset over what you don't have is to waste what you do have.

Ken S. Keyes, Jr.

Popcorn Balls

Serves 8

5 quarts popped popcorn
2 C granulated sugar
1½ C water
½ tsp salt
½ C Karo® light corn syrup
1 tsp GF apple cider vinegar
1 tsp GF vanilla

Place popcorn in large roasting pan or large bowl.

Coat sides of large saucepan with GF margarine. Combine sugar, water, salt, corn syrup and vinegar.

Cook, without stirring to hard ball stage (250 degrees). Remove from heat and stir in vanilla.

Pour hot syrup over popcorn in a thin stream. Stir with wooden spoon to coat all kernels.

Coat hands with GF margarine and form popcorn into balls. Be careful not to burn yourself as syrup is very hot.

Wrap each popcorn ball in plastic wrap and store in airtight container.

Creamy Mints

Makes 2 dozen mints

1 lb powdered sugar
½ C GF, DF margarine, softened
1/3 C Karo® light syrup
GF peppermint flavoring to taste
GF food colors

In large bowl combine powdered sugar, margarine and Karo® syrup until partially mixed. Knead with hands until completely mixed and smooth.

Put 1 – 2 drops peppermint flavoring on mixture. Knead until thoroughly incorporated.

Divide into 3 – 4 parts. Add 2 – 3 drops GF food coloring to each part – different colors to each section. Knead until color is fully incorporated.

Pinch off a small piece of mixture, about the size of a large marble. Roll into a ball and flatten on waxed paper with fingers. Continue to form mints until all mixture has been used.

You can flatten mint balls with a fork for a different texture.

Leave mints out overnight to dry. Store in airtight container.

Happy Snacks

Makes 4 smiles

1 apple
Homemade Marshmallows, cut
    into ¼" squares
GF peanut butter

*Recipe for Homemade
marshmallows on page 148)

Cut apple in half and then in half again. Cut our core from each piece. Slice each quarter in half.

Spread peanut butter on one side of each apple slice. Top four of the slices with marshmallow pieces. (Line them up like teeth.)

Put other apple slice on top of the marshmallows, forming a "smile".

You haven't lost your smile at all. It's right under your nose. You just forgot it was there.

Anonymous

Puppy Chow

Makes 6 cups

1 C GF peanut butter
½ C GF margarine
1 -12oz pkg carob chips
 (or dairy-free chocolate chips)
2 C powdered sugar
6 C GF square rice cereal

1 large brown paper bag.

Put cereal in large bowl and set aside.

Put powdered sugar in large brown paper bag.

In medium saucepan, melt peanut butter, margarine and carob chips over low heat just until melted.

Pour melted carob (or chocolate) over cereal and stir gently to combine, until cereal is coated.

Pour chocolate covered cereal into paper bag. Roll top closed and shake until completely coated with powdered sugar.

Place coated cereal in airtight container to store.

Cream Puffs

Makes 12 puffs

1 C water
½ C GF margarine
1/3 C potato starch flour
1/3 C rice flour
1/3 C tapioca flour
½ tsp salt
1 Tbl granulated sugar
4 eggs

Preheat oven to 450 degrees. Grease cookie sheet.

Combine water and GF margarine in medium saucepan. Bring to a rapid boil. In medium bowl mix flours, salt and sugar. Add all at one time to boiling water. Stir vigorously until mixture forms a ball that leaves sides of pan. Remove from heat and cool slightly.

Add eggs, one at a time, beating well (with wooden spoon or electric mixer) after each egg.

Drop 12 spoonfuls onto prepared cookie sheet. Bake at 450 degrees for 20 minutes, then reduce heat to 350 degrees and bake for 20 minutes more. Remove from oven and prick with knife to let steam escape.

Serve cold with dairy-free whipped topping.

Meringue Cookies

Makes 1 dozen cookies

3 egg whites
¼ tsp GF cream of tartar
¾ C granulated sugar

Parchment paper cut to size of cookie sheet

Preheat oven to 275 degrees.

In medium glass or stainless steel bowl (do not use plastic) beat together egg whites and cream of tartar until foamy. Gradually beat in sugar on high, a little at a time, until mixture is very stiff and glossy.

Drop 12 spoonfuls onto brown paper place on cookie sheet.

Bake for 1 hour. Turn off oven and leave meringues in oven until oven is cool. (You can leave them in the oven overnight.)

Store cookies in air tight container.

Yellow Cake

Makes 1 cake

10 eggs, separated
¾ C granulated sugar
½ C granulated sugar
½ C tapioca flour
½ C potato starch flour
1 tsp xanthan gum

Preheat oven to 350 degrees. Grease Bundt cake pan or angel food pan and dust with sugar.

In small bowl combine flours and xanthan gum.

In large bowl, beat egg whites until foamy. Slowly add 3/4 cup sugar and beat on high until stiff peaks.

In medium bowl beat egg yolks with 1/2 cup sugar until smooth, about 2 minutes.

Fold beaten egg yolks into beaten egg whites. Fold flour mixture into egg mixture, just enough to distribute flour throughout egg mixture.

Bake for 1 hour, or until knife inserted in center comes out clean.

You are never too old to set another goal or to dream a new dream

C.S. Lewis

Flaky Pie Crust

Makes 1 pie crust

¾ C tapioca flour
¼ C potato starch flour
½ tsp salt
1/3 C GF, DF margarine
2 - 3 Tbl warm water
2 Tbl soy milk
1 egg

In large bowl mix dry ingredients. Cut in GF margarine using two knives or a pastry cutter until it looks like fine meal. Add water gradually until dough forms a ball. (Better to have it wet than crumbly and dry.) Form dough into a ball and wrap in plastic wrap. Let it sit on counter for 30 minutes.

Dust counter or pastry sheet with tapioca flour. Roll out dough so it is 1" larger than size of pie pan. Gently lift pie crust (on rolling pin) and place in pie pan. Fold excess pie crust under, around edge of pie pan. Crimp edges with fingers.

Fill crust with pumpkin filling (previous page). Cover edges of pie crust with aluminum foil.

In small bowl, mix soy milk and egg. Remove foil at last 10 minutes of baking and brush crust with egg mixture. Bake 10 minutes to brown crust.

Serve with dairy-free whipped topping or GF soy ice cream.

White Bundt Cake

Serves 6

¾ C rice flour
½ C tapioca flour
¼ C potato starch flour
¼ C cornstarch
1 C granulated sugar
1 egg
1 C soy milk
1 tsp vinegar
½ C vegetable oil

¼ C granulated sugar

Preheat oven to 350 degrees. Grease Bundt cake pan. Coat bottom and sides of pan with 1/4 cup sugar. (This prevents cake from sticking to pan.)

In large mixing bowl, combine oil and 1 cup sugar. Add egg and mix completely. Add soy milk and vinegar. Stir until completely combined.

In small separate bowl, mix flours and cornstarch to combine. Add flour mixture to liquid mixture in large bowl. Stir just to combine.

Pour mixture into prepared pan. Bake 45 - 55 minutes. Cake is done when top springs back when pressed lightly.

Suggestion

Frost with Boiled Frosting (page 159)

Slice and spread with dairy free whipped topping

Slice and spread with dairy-free chocolate pudding

Homemade Marshmallows

Serves 6 – 8

4 pkgs unflavored gelatin
1 C cold water
2 C sugar
2 egg whites
2 C GF powdered sugar, sifted
parchment paper

In large bowl, beat egg whites until stiff peaks and then fold in the sifted powdered sugar. While mixer is on low, slowly poor in the cooled gelatin mixture. Increase speed and beat until white and beat until white and thick. Mixture should double in size.

Pour marshmallow mixture onto lined cookie sheet. Dust with more sifted powdered sugar, covering completely. Leave out overnight or for at lease 3 hours to set. Marshmallows should be light and springy when set.

Line a cookie sheet with sides with parchment paper. Heavily coat with sifted powdered sugar, covering paper completely.

In medium saucepan, soak the gelatin in water, stirring until soft (about 5 minutes). Add sugar and gently dissolve over low heat, about 5 minutes. Remove from heat and allow to cool until next step is completed.

Move slab of marshmallows on parchment paper to counter. Using a large knife, slice marshmallows into 2" squares. This is best accomplished by sliding tip of knife through marshmallows from one end of parchment paper to the other, rather than cutting in a sawing motion. Peel marshmallow squares off parchment paper. Store in airtight container or zip lock bags.

Citrus Sponge Cake

Makes 1 cake

½ C potato starch
½ C cornstarch
1 tsp GF baking powder
½ tsp salt
½ tsp xanthan gum
5 egg yolks
5 egg whites
¾ C granulated sugar
¼ C orange juice
1 tsp GF vanilla
1 tsp grated lemon rind
  (optional)
½ tsp GF cream of tartar

Preheat over to 325 degrees.

Thoroughly mix potato starch, cornstarch, baking powder, salt and xanthan gum.

In separate bowl, beat egg yolks and sugar with electric mixer until thick and lemon colored.

Add orange juice, GF vanilla and lemon rind. Mix until just blended. Add dry ingredients and mix until combined, being careful not to overbeat mixture.

In small bowl, beat egg whites with cream of tartar until stiff peaks. Fold egg white mixture into batter until just blended.

Pour into an ungreased 10 inch tube pan and bake for 40 minutes. Then turn up heat to 350 degrees for 5-10 minutes and bake until top is lightly browned.

Remove pan from oven and flip over on counter. Leave flipped over until completely cooled. Refrigerate unused cake.

Gingerbread

Serves 4

½ C light or dark bean flour
½ C cornstarch
¼ C tapioca flour
1 tsp GF baking soda
1 tsp GF cinnamon
½ tsp GF ginger
½ tsp GF nutmeg
¼ tsp xanthan gum
½ C granulated sugar
¼ C honey
4 Tbl vegetable oil
½ C boiling water
2 eggs

¼ C granulated sugar

Preheat oven to 350 degrees. Grease an 8" square cake pan with vegetable oil. Sprinkle 1/4 cup sugar in pan, tipping pan to coat bottom & sides with 1/4 cup sugar.

In medium bowl, combine flours, cornstarch, baking soda, spices and xanthan gum.

In large mixing bowl, combine 1/2 cup sugar, honey, oil, water and eggs. Stir to combine. Add flour mixture and beat well. Pour batter into prepared pan and bake 30 - 40 minutes, or until a knife inserted in center comes out clean.

Serve with GF dairy-free whipped topping.

Be brave. Take risks. Nothing can substitute experience.

Paulo Coelho

Baked Apples

Serves 4

4 medium apples
4 Tbl GF margarine
½ C GF brown sugar
2 tsp GF cinnamon
½ C water

Preheat oven to 350 degrees. Grease sides and bottom of pie pan. Set aside.

Cut out core of apple ALMOST to bottom of apple. Do NOT cut through bottom of apple. (I use a small melon ball tool.)

In small bowl, combine GF brown sugar and cinnamon. Pack core of each apple with brown sugar mixture, leaving 1/4" at top. Place 1 Tbl GF margarine on top of brown sugar mixture in each apple. Place apples in pie pan. Pour water in pie pan. Cover apples with aluminum foil. Bake for 20 - 30 minutes until apples are tender.

Suggestion

Serve with GF soy ice cream
Serve with GF dairy-free whipped topping.

Lemon Pudding

Serves 4

3 eggs
Juice of 1 lemon
1 C granulated sugar
1 C soy milk
2 Tbl cornstarch

Preheat oven to 325 degrees.

Separate eggs into 2 small bowls. Set aside.

In large bowl beat egg yolks until light yellow. Add sugar and beat until pale yellow, about 5 minutes.

Add lemon juice and cornstarch. Beat well. Add soy milk and beat well. Set aside.

In medium bowl beat egg whites until stiff peaks form. Fold egg whites into egg yolk mixture.

Pour pudding into an 8" x 8" ungreased casserole pan. Place casserole pan in larger pan with 2" of water in it.

Bake for 40 – 50 minutes until set.

Banana Pudding

Serves 4

¾ C granulated sugar
1/8 C tapioca flour
1 Tbl cornstarch
½ tsp salt
2 ½ C soy milk
4 egg yolks
1 Tbl GF margarine
2 tsp GF vanilla
4 bananas, cut into ¼" slices

In medium saucepan, mix sugar, flour, corn starch, egg and salt. Set aside. In separate medium saucepan, heat soy milk until steaming, but not boiling.

Slowly pour milk into saucepan with dry ingredients, whisking constantly. Whisk until smooth.

Place pan over medium heat and cook, whisking constantly until mixture is very thick. Continue to cook for 2 – 3 minutes, continuing to stir with whisk.

Remove from heat and stir in margarine, vanilla and bananas. Spoon pudding into serving dishes and refrigerate until cool.

I've been there – that's why I'm here.

Anonymous

Sea Foam Candy

Makes 4 dozen squares

3 C granulated sugar
½ C Karo® light syrup
2 egg whites
1 tsp GF vanilla
½ tsp salt
1 C chopped pecans
2/3 C water

Grease 13 x 9" cake pan with GF, DF margarine.

In large saucepan combine sugar, syrup and water. Heat to a rolling boil. Continue to boil without stirring to hard ball stage.

While syrup is boiling, beat egg whites and salt in large bowl until stiff peaks form.

When syrup has reached hard ball stage, remove from heat. With beaters on high, pour syrup in a thin stream into egg whites.

Continue to beat until firm enough to hold its shape, about 10 – 15 minutes. Add vanilla and mix 1 minute more.

Pour into prepared pan. When cool, cut into squares, 6 across and 8 down.

Holiday Cereal Mix

Serves 8

1½ C GF square rice cereal
1½ C GF square corn cereal
2 C GF pretzels
1 C salted peanuts (optional)
½ C GF,DF margarine
2 Tbl GF Worcestershire sauce
1-½ tsp Lawry's seasoned salt
¼ tsp GF garlic powder

Preheat oven to 275 degrees.

In large roasting pan, combine cereal, pretzels and peanuts. Set aside.

In small saucepan combine margarine, Worcestershire sauce, seasoned salt and garlic salt. Cook on low heat, stirring constantly, until margarine is melted and seasonings are combined.

Pour margarine mixture over cereal mixture, stirring to coat.

Bake for 40 minutes, stirring occasionally.

Store in airtight container.

Chocolate Chews

Makes 5 dozen 2" cookies

1 C rice flour
½ C potato starch flour
¼ C cornstarch
½ tsp xanthan gum
½ tsp GF baking soda
2/3 C vegetable oil
1½ C granulated sugar
1 tsp GF vanilla
2 Tbl soy milk
1 egg
1/3 C cocoa powder
1 C walnuts or pecans (optional)

Preheat oven to 350 degrees. Lightly grease 2 cookie sheets.

In a medium bowl add flours, cornstarch, xanthan gum and baking soda. Add cocoa to dry mixture and stir until combined.

In large mixing bowl, blend oil and egg. Add sugar and beat until fluffy. Add vanilla and milk and mix well.

Add the dry mixture into the wet ingredients. Stir just until combined. Add nuts and stir to distribute nuts.

Drop by rounded teaspoonfuls onto prepared cookie sheets. Bake 10 - 12 minutes. Let cookie sheet sit on top of stove for a few minutes before removing from pan.

Dairy-Free Chocolate Pudding

Makes 2½ cups

3 Tbl cornstarch
2 Tbl water
1½ C soy milk
¼ tsp GF vanilla
¼ C granulated sugar
¼ C unsweetened cocoa
powder

In large saucepan stir together soy milk, GF vanilla, sugar, cocoa, cornstarch and water. Heat over medium heat, stirring constantly until mixture boils.

Continue to cook and stir until mixture thickens. Remove from heat. Pudding will continue to thicken as it cools. Allow to cool five minutes, then chill in refrigerator until completely cool.

Serve with non-dairy, GF whipped topping.

When you know better, you do better.

Anonymous

Boiled Frosting

Frosts one cake

1½ C granulated sugar
¼ tsp GF cream of tartar
2/3 C boiling water
2 egg whites
1 tsp GF vanilla

In a large, heavy saucepan mix sugar with cream of tartar. Add boiling water, stirring until sugar is dissolved.

Bring mixture to a boil, over medium heat. Boil rapidly, without stirring, for 10 minutes (soft ball stage – 240 degrees)

Remove mixture from heat and set aside while you beat the egg whites.

In large bowl beat egg whites until stiff. Slowly pour a thin stream of syrup into egg whites, beating constantly with electric mixer.

Continue to beat frosting until frosting has cooled to warm and is of spreading consistency.

Stir in vanilla.

Frost cake immediately, or refrigerate frosting until ready to use.

Crunchy Honey Snack

Serves 4

4 C GF square rice cereal
½ C GF pretzels
1 C pecans
1/3 C GF margarine
½ tsp GF cinnamon
¼ C honey

Preheat oven to 350 degrees.

In large bowl combine cereal, pretzels, pecans and cinnamon. Set aside.

In small saucepan combine GF margarine and honey. Heat on low, stirring constantly to combine.

Pour honey mixture over cereal mixture, stirring to coat. Spread mixture on large cookie sheet.

Bake for 12 to 16 minutes or until lightly glazed, stirring occasionally.

Remove from oven and spread on waxed paper to cool. Store in airtight container.

Flourless Peanut Butter Cookies

Makes 2 dozen

2 eggs
1 C GF peanut butter (chunky or
creamy)
1 C granulated sugar

Preheat oven to 350 degrees.

Grease cookie sheet.

In medium bowl beat eggs until light yellow. Stir in sugar and peanut butter.

Drop by spoonfuls onto cookie sheet, 2" apart. Press flat using a fork.

Bake 10 – 12 minutes or until lightly brown around edges. Cookie should spring back a little when pressed in the center.

Everyday may not be good, but there's something good in every day.

Anonymous

Drop Sugar Cookies

Makes 3 dozen 2" cookies

1 C GF margarine
¾ C soy flour
¾ C potato starch flour
1¼ C tapioca flour
¼ C granulated sugar
1½ C GF powdered sugar
2½ tsp xanthan gum
1 egg
1 tsp GF baking soda
1 tsp GF cream of tartar

Preheat oven to 350 degrees.

In large bowl cream together margarine, granulated sugar and powdered sugar. Add egg and beat until blended.

Add baking soda, cream of tartar, soy flour and tapioca flour. Mix until well blended.

Add tapioca flour and xanthan gum. Mix with hands until dry ingredients are mixed and dough is thick and holds together.

Take a tablespoon of dough and form into ball. Place balls of dough on ungreased, non-stick cookie sheet. Flatten balls slightly with fingers.

Bake for 10 – 12 minutes or until edges begin to brown. Remove cookies from oven and cool for 5 minutes on cookie sheet. Remove cookies and cool completely on paper towels or brown paper.

Creamy Pumpkin Custard

Serves 8

1-15oz can pumpkin
1 C soy milk
2 Tbl melted GF margarine
2 Tbl tapioca flour
½ C GF brown sugar
¼ C granulated sugar
2 eggs
½ tsp salt
2 tsp GF cinnamon
1½ tsp GF nutmeg
½ tsp GF ground cloves

Preheat oven to 350 degrees.

Place cupcake papers in 8 large or 12 small sections in cupcake pan.

In large bowl mix all liquid ingredients until well blended.

In small bowl combine all dry ingredients.

Slowly whisk dry ingredients into wet ingredients. Whip until smooth. Fill cupcake papers ¾ full. Smooth top of filling.

Bake for 20 minutes until knife inserted in center comes out clean.

Serve warm with non-dairy whipped topping.

Suggestion:

Custard can also be baked in greased 8" x 8" casserole pan. Bake 30 – 35 minutes or until knife inserted in center comes out clean.

Old Fashioned Taffy Pull

Makes 48 one inch pieces

¾ C water
2 C granulated sugar
1¼ C Karo® light corn syrup
2 Tbl GF, DF margarine
1 tsp salt
2 tsp GF vanilla

The more hands you have to make taffy, the easier it will be to get all of it rolled, cut and wrapped. "The more the merrier" especially with taffy pulling!

In large, heavy saucepan combine water, sugar and corn syrup. Heat over medium heat, stirring until sugar is dissolved.

Continue to cook mixture, without stirring, until it reaches soft ball stage (240 degrees).

Grease a large cookie sheet with GF margarine. Pour vanilla into hot syrup and stir until combined. Pour hot syrup onto cookie sheet.

Using a wooden paddle or wooden spoon, lift edges of hot taffy and pull to center. Continue to pull edges of taffy into center until taffy cools slightly.

Butter hands and pull taffy, stretching and folding it back on itself. Taffy will begin to turn white.

Continue to pull taffy until it begins to get stiff. Divide taffy into 8 pieces. Roll the first piece into rope about ½" wide. Using a sharp, oiled knife, cut taffy rope into ½ - 1" pieces. Wrap each piece in small squares of waxed paper.

Roll and cut additional pieces of taffy and wrap in waxed paper. Store in airtight container. Taffy will keep for up to 2 weeks.

Candy Canes

Serves 8

¾ C water
2 C granulated sugar
1-¼ C Karo® light corn syrup
2 Tbl GF margarine
1 tsp salt
2 tsp GF vanilla
5 drops GF red food color
5 – 10 drops GF peppermint extract

In large, heavy saucepan combine water, sugar and corn syrup. Heat over medium heat, stirring until sugar is dissolved.

Continue to cook mixture, without stirring, until it reaches soft crack stage (270 degrees).

Grease 2 large cookie sheets with GF margarine. Pour half the syrup onto each cookie sheet. Stir food coloring and extract into sheet of taffy.

Using a wooden paddle or wooden spoon, lift edges of hot taffy and pull to center. Continue to pull edges of taffy into center until taffy color and flavoring are incorporated.

Butter hands and pull taffy, stretching and folding it back on itself. Uncolored taffy will begin to turn white. Red taffy will lighten in color.

Continue to pull taffy until it begins to get stiff. Divide each piece of taffy into 4 pieces. Roll the first piece into rope about ¼" wide. Lay one white rope next to one red rope. Gently twist double rope until colors twirl around each other. Roll double rope until smooth so it looks like a straight candy cane.

Cut taffy ropes into 5" to 6" pieces. Curl top to form cane. Set aside while you roll remaining candy canes.

Wrap each candy cane in wax paper or plastic wrap. Store in airtight container. Candy canes will keep for up to 2 weeks.

Banana Cream Pie

Serves 8

2 C soy milk
2/3 C granulated sugar
¼ C tapioca starch flour
1 tsp xanthan gum
¼ tsp salt
2 eggs
½ tsp GF vanilla
2 bananas, peeled and sliced
1 GF baked pie crust

In large bowl combine dry ingredients. Add eggs and vanilla and beat well. Set aside.

In large saucepan, heat soy milk on low. Remove from heat. Pour egg mixture into hot milk, stirring constantly with wooden spoon. Bring to a slow boil, stirring constantly. Boil for one minute.

Fold banana slices into pie mixture. Pour mixture into baked pie crust. Refrigerate until cold.

Serve with GF non-dairy whipped topping.

The doors we open and close each day decide the lives we live.

Flora Whitmore

Thin Crispy Sugar Cookies

Makes 2 dozen

1½ C GF powdered sugar
1 C GF margarine
¾ C soy flour
¾ C potato starch flour
½ C tapioca flour
1 egg
1 tsp GF baking soda
1 tsp GF cream of tartar
2 tsp xanthan gum

Preheat oven to 350 degrees.

In large bowl combine margarine and powdered sugar. Mix until combined. Add egg and mix for 2 minutes.

Add flours, baking soda and cream of tartar. Mix until dry ingredients are combined.

Add xanthan gum and mix for 2 minutes using mixer, wooden spoon or hands.

Drop dough by heaping spoonfuls onto ungreased non-stick cookie sheet. Leave 2" – 3" between cookies as cookies will flatten and spread as they bake.

Bake for 10 – 12 minutes until cookies have spread and are beginning to brown around edges. Remove cookie sheet from oven. Allow cookies to cool for 5 minutes on cookie sheet. Remove from cookie sheet and cool completely on wire rack or parchment paper.

Store in airtight container.

Powdered Sugar Frosting

Makes 1 cup

2 C GF powdered sugar
3 Tbl softened GF margarine
3-5 Tbl soy milk
1 tsp GF vanilla

GF food colors

In large bowl combine powdered sugar and 3 Tbl soy milk. Stir with wooden spoon to combine.

Add vanilla and margarine and stir until smooth. If frosting is too dry add more soy milk one tsp at a time until desired consistency.

Divide frosting into separate bowls and add food coloring a few drops at a time. Stir until food coloring is incorporated.

Use this frosting to frost cut-out cookies or put between 2 GF crackers for a quick treat.

CHAPTER 13

Miscellaneous

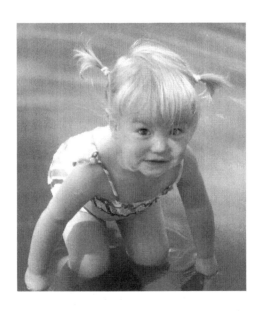

Measurements

3 teaspoons	=	1 Tablespoon
4 Tablespoons	=	¼ cup
8 Tablespoons	=	½ cup
12 Tablespoons	=	¾ cup
16 Tablespoons	=	1 cup
2 cups	=	1 pint
4 cups	=	1 quart
4 quarts	=	1 gallon
16 ounces	=	1 pound
32 ounces	=	1 quart
1 ounce liquid	=	2 Tablespoons
8 ounces liquid	=	1 cup

Abbreviations

GF	=	Gluten-free
DF	=	Dairy-free
tsp	=	Teaspoon
Tbl	=	Tablespoon
C	=	Cup

Types of rice

Long Grain White Rice
Has a long, slender kernel four to five times longer than its width. Rice kernels do not cling together well.

Medium Grain White Rice
Has a shorter, wider kernel two to three times longer than its width. It has a tendency to cling together better than long grain rice.

Short Grain White Rice
Has a short, plump, almost round kernel. The rice grains are soft and cling together well.

Sweet or Waxy White Rice
Is short and plump with a chalky white kernel. When cooked, it loses its shape and is very glutinous (does NOT contain gluten). The starch and rice flour from sweet rice is used in frozen products as a binder because it doesn't break down during freezing and thawing.

Aromatic White Rice
Have a flavor and aroma similar to that of roasted nuts or popcorn. The most popular are:

Della - which cooks dry, separate and is fluffy
Jasmine - which cooks moist and clings together
Basmati - which swells only lengthwise and cooks into
very long, slender grains which are dry, separate and fluffy
Arborio - has a characteristic white dot at the center of each grain. It is a large rice grain which develops a creamy texture around a chewy center. It has an exceptional ability to absorb flavors and is used in risotto.

Brown Rice

Only the hull has been removed from brown rice. It has a slightly chewy texture and a nutty flavor. The brown color is caused by the bran layers which are rich in minerals and vitamins.

Types of Potatoes

Yukon Gold

Yellow potatoes that are considered "all purpose" which means you can cook and bake them. They have a somewhat softer flesh when boiled.

Red Potatoes

Best used for steaming, boiling, roasting, au gratin, scalloped

Russet Potatoes

These are high in starch. They are an "all purpose" potato and can be used for boiling or baking. This is the most commonly used potato.

White Rose

These are low in starch. They are good for boiling and stay firm and hold their shape after cooking.

Fingerling Potatoes

These are "finger-shaped" and are low in starch. They are best used for baking, boiling and roasting.

Russian Blue

Also knows as "purple potatoes" they are medium in starch. Best used for baking, boiling and steaming. Use them to make purple mashed potatoes or french fries.

Don't Feed Me, LLC

Allergy Alert Pins

Allergy Alert Pins are a safe solution to alerting others that your child has food allergies. Bracelets and necklaces can pose a hazard for small children. Our pins have a no-snag jeweler's pin and safety clasp. Our pins are also available with an adhesive backing to provide an easy, safe way to attach the button to clothing on very small children.

Special orders for allergies not listed are available at NO EXTRA CHARGE. Please visit our website at www.dontfeedme.com to see full-color samples or to place an order.

Allergy Alert Clothing
For Children with Food Allergies

Medical Alert bracelets and necklaces are too big for infants and small children and can be a very real safety issue. Caregivers may not always read them, thinking they are just pretty jewelry.

When my granddaughter, Aivah, was diagnosed with Gluten and Casein allergies, we discovered just how difficult it was to make others aware of the danger of feeding her the wrong foods. We realized there are many other families with the same concerns for their children.

We created **"Don't Feed Me" Allergy Alert Clothing** for infants and small children. Each item of clothing screen-printed and is designed for a specific food allergy.

I encourage you to visit our website to see how our clothing is helping one small child. Help us to help others like Aivah.

Visit us at www.dontfeedme.com to see color samples of our shirts or to place an order.

Cookbook Orders

Additional copies of this cookbook can be ordered through our website at www.dontfeedme.com, at **Amazon.com** or **BarnesandNoble.com**

You can also order a cookbook by sending us an email at info@dontfeedme.com.

Index